CAN STATE UNIVERSITIES BE MANAGED?

CAN STATE UNIVERSITIES BE MANAGED?

A Primer for Presidents and Management Teams

Duane Acker

Foreword by Harold Wechsler

AMERICAN COUNCIL ON EDUCATION
PRAEGER
Series on Higher Education

Library of Congress Cataloging-in-Publication Data

Acker, Duane.
    Can state universities be managed? : a primer for presidents and management teams /
Duane Acker ; foreword by Harold Wechsler.
        p. cm.—(ACE/Praeger series on higher education)
    Includes bibliographical references and index.
    ISBN 0–275–99193–8 (alk. paper)
    1. College administrators—United States. 2. Universities and colleges—United States—
Administration. I. Title.
    LB2341.A27` 2006
    379.1′01—dc22   2006021004

British Library Cataloguing in Publication Data is available.

Library of Congress Catalog Card Number: 2006021004
ISBN: 0–275–99193–8

First published in 2006

Praeger Publishers, 88 Post Road West, Westport, CT 06881
An imprint of Greenwood Publishing Group, Inc.
www.praeger.com

Printed in the United States of America

The paper used in this book complies with the
Permanent Paper Standard issued by the National
Information Standards Organization (Z39.48-1984).

10 9 8 7 6 5 4 3 2 1

CONTENTS

FOREWORD

Can State Universities Be Managed? invites readers to contemplate careers in administrative leadership. Drawing from knowledge acquired as president of Kansas State University, and from his multifarious experiences at other universities and in government service, Duane Acker takes us through the cycle of a presidency—from the decision to apply, to life after resignation. Aspirants for high academic office, he notes, must carefully evaluate whether their ability, preparation, and energy level square with the institution's current mission and needs. They must also assess their willingness to work with multiple constituencies to identify and realize its future promise. Congruence between individuals and institutions, he concludes, may not be permanent—universities and individuals move on. But the match is best realized when presidents, provosts, deans, and chairs recognize that the significant state investment calls for scholarship and service to the state's citizens as well as to educating the university's resident students.

Talented individuals can do many things with their lives; Duane Acker urges novices to consider the intangible rewards of high-level administration and seeks to persuade seasoned administrators that a university presidency is a special calling. Full of insight and bereft of clichés, the succinct chapters in this book address—and often demystify—issues likely to concern aspirants, while alerting them to unanticipated opportunities and problems. It does not shirk from difficult issues—burnout and the possible costs to family life, for example. But its upbeat tone suggests strategies for working through potential drawbacks. Especially apt is the reminder to cultivate a life outside the university. Personal friendships; devotion to family; and community, religious, and corporate service can allay the burdens of administration, while these activities may provide ideas and contacts that redound to the office and institution.

Scholars will profit from President Acker's ability to shed light on many areas of current research on higher education—defining the roles of the president and central administration in decentralized universities; integrating academic and extracurricular life; increasing access to postsecondary education, and balancing institutional autonomy and community responsiveness, for example. Perhaps most important: he offers creative suggestions for honoring the tradition and history of a university while marshalling its strengths and resources to effect salutary change.

Can State Universities Be Managed? reminds us that the university presidency is a stewardship, not a sinecure. A president leads by example: selfless, honest personal conduct is a *sine qua non* for proper institutional behavior. Accountability is not an abstraction: it implies prudent use of resources—provided by others—to prepare the next generation for life in a complex world.

For the public, this book candidly and affectionately describes the ways that colleges and universities function—and how to make these national assets work better.

Enjoy!

Harold Wechsler
Professor of Education
New York University

PREFACE

A new president of a college or university, or a new member of the president's management team, needs a clear perspective of the institution and its system, a solid knowledge base about that institution or unit thereof, and an understanding of the importance and symbolism of certain early actions in their administrative roles. In their respective roles, presidents and other administrators delegate, innovate, coach, and give feedback; they are concerned about enrollment, funding, and relationships with media and the community. Each of these important topics, and many more, are addressed in this book.

My goal in writing this book is to help university managers, from president to department head or center director, to be fully prepared to establish missions and goals and to effectively lead their pursuit. I want each to avoid some of the pitfalls, to be able to anticipate and confidently handle issues and circumstances they will confront. It is my hope and expectation this book will contribute to those ends.

The target audiences for this book are:

1. New or potential university and college presidents;
2. New or potential deans, department heads or chairs, provosts, vice presidents, and others in academic leadership and management; and
3. Those who see state universities—or any college or university—as a valuable resource for their children, their industries or professions, and for society as a whole. This latter group may include trustees, donors, alumni, industry or community leaders, and government officials.

My overarching purpose in writing the book, as in teaching a class or preparing materials for an extension program, is to present useful information and concepts illustrated with real-life examples. I have drawn from the experiences and wisdom of others, especially trustees, presidents and provosts, as well as from my own in five state universities: as a faculty member, associate dean, research and extension director, dean, vice chancellor, and president.

I have also drawn from my experiences in two federal agencies and in the private sector. Coupled with international work and continuing university relationships as a collaborative professor, committee member, and client, these experiences gave me a broader perspective of university management than I had as president. They also gave me stronger motives to write this book. I see the university management task as increasingly challenging in the twenty-first century.

Primacy in the subtitle is given to the president and much of the writing will be directed to a potential or new president. Regardless, a new provost, vice president, dean, or other administrator may substitute their title and circumstance, and, I hope, will find the advice and illustrations useful. In some of the writing, I will be giving advice and sharing experiences as a former president. In other sections, the advice and illustrations will come from my experience as a dean, or from some other role.

For those few sections that seem almost exclusive to a president's concern, sensitivity to those presidential circumstances and responsibility may help provosts and others see more fully their role as a member of the management team and their support relationship to the president.

For the third audience, such as trustees, government officials, or university supporters, I hope the book will provide a broad understanding and acceptance of the important management responsibilities held by those chosen to be presidents, provosts, vice presidents, deans, and department heads or chairs. This information may be especially useful to members of search-and-screening committees and, because of their key role in "participatory management," to faculty leadership.

Although state universities are highlighted in the title of this book, all colleges and universities—public, private, four-year, two-year, liberal arts, or technology—share many features. All focus on student learning and growth, a search for the truth, and service to their respective disciplines and communities. All exist in a very public environment, and all carry management challenges.

Similarly, though my university employment experience has been with U.S. state universities, principles and illustrations will hold for and apply to the management circumstances of provincial, state, and federal universities of Canada and other countries too.

For simplicity in writing, except for a cited or quoted person with the title of chancellor, I have used the term president in referring to a campus head, whether the campus is an independent institution or one of a multi-campus university. And, except for a cited or quoted person with the title of regent, I have used the term trustee.

A variety of terms are used in universities and colleges to describe linking the intellectual resources or research outcomes to clientele who are not resident students—Extension, Continuing Education, Service, Outreach, Technology Transfer, and Engagement. To me, the word Extension embraces all of those categories and is university-wide, and so I have used that term. However, I urge the reader to substitute the term that is most meaningful in his or her circumstance.

May these pages be of help to the reader and, through the reader, of particular help to one of society's major assets, the state university.

Duane Acker

ACKNOWLEDGMENTS

The first person who encouraged me to proceed with this work was Ralph Titus, the long-time "Radio Voice" of Kansas State University, after he had led me through the first of several intended oral history sessions. A month later, I mentioned the idea to Ohio State University Trustee Jim Patterson and Purdue University Regent John Hardin. One responded, "It's needed!" The other, "Do it!" And each followed up with suggestions.

More encouragement and suggestions came from President Peter Magrath of the National Association of State Universities and Land Grant Colleges (NASULGC); President Richard T (Tom) Ingram of the Association of Governing Boards of Universities and Colleges; President Emeritus Joseph Crowley, University of Nevada, Reno; President Emeritus John Byrne of Oregon State University; Provost Michael Hogan, University of Iowa; and former colleague, Chancellor Emeritus Gene Budig, University of Kansas.

Whose perspective of state university management could be more useful than that of experienced and dedicated members of governing boards? Valuable inputs came from current and former governing board members Karen Hendricks, a colleague of Jim Patterson on The Ohio State Board of Trustees; Nelson Galle, Kansas Board of Regents; Edwin Turner, University of Missouri Board of Curators; Tom Lyon, University of Wisconsin Board of Regents; Richard Rominger, University of California Board of Regents; and Michael Gartner and Jim Tyler, Iowa Board of Regents. Each was most generous with both their time and their insight.

Peter Mcpherson, President Emeritus of Michigan State University and recently named to replace retiring Magrath at NASULGC, gave me an hour at the end of a long day less than 24 hours after a flight from Africa. Penn State President Graham Spanier, New Mexico State President Mike Martin, and University of Nebraska-Lincoln Chancellor Harvey Perlman each offered suggestions for content.

David Smith, Chancellor of the Texas Tech University System and former president of the Texas Tech Health Sciences Center gave me a generous short course for the chapter, Medical Schools and Teaching Hospitals, and Professor Harold Wechsler of the Steinhardt School of Education at New York University did the same for the chapter, Faculty and Staff Unions. Professor Wechsler also accepted our invitation to write the foreword for the book.

My current associations with Iowa State University as a collaborative professor and member of several advisory groups provided convenient access to considerable help from Warren Madden, Vice President for Finance; Stanley Johnson, Vice Provost for Extension; Sonja Klocker, Assistant to the Vice Provost for Research; and Steven Carter, Director of the University Research Park and also of the Pappajohn Entrepreneurship Center.

Valuable information and suggestions also came from Tom Rawson, Vice President for Finance at Kansas State University; Sandra and Clay Edwards, Associate Vice Chancellors for Development at the University of Arkansas; Stephen Kimata, Assistant Vice President for Finance at the University of Virginia; Francille Firebaugh, Vice Provost at Cornell University; Robert Easter, Dean of Agriculture, Consumer, and Environmental Sciences at the University of Illinois; and Howard Tuckman, Dean of the Rutgers University Business School.

Special thanks goes to Carol J. Peterson, Provost and Vice President of Academic Affairs at South Dakota State University; Owen Koeppe, my former provost at Kansas State University; and Richard Seaton, Kansas State University Counsel for their willingness to review and offer comments on major sections of the manuscript.

I also express appreciation for the privilege of working under and with—and learning from—a good many presidents, vice presidents, deans, associate deans, and department heads on five campuses; cabinet and subcabinet officers in Washington; university officers and institute directors with whom I worked globally in consulting and program review assignments; and executives in the private sector. Each has contributed to my perspective of university leadership and management.

I thank the American Council on Education (ACE) for including this work in its series on higher education and, especially, ACE Executive Editor Susan Slesinger, whose generous encouragement, advice and sound judgment guided me through the process toward publication. Thanks also to Bharath Parthasarathy, Dennis Troutman and their colleagues for handling the copy edit and other production tasks in a timely manner. My work with each has been a pleasant experience.

No acknowledgment would be adequate without highlighting my wife, Shirley, my partner and a generous hostess to and highly appreciated friend of students, faculty, staff, alumni, legislators, and many others throughout our university and government years.

Duane Acker

PART I

Perspectives

One of my predecessors at Kansas State University, Milton Eisenhower, wrote that when offered the presidency of then Kansas State College, he and his wife listed all the factors for and against accepting the presidency. What tipped the balance to accept "was my belief that at last I would have the opportunity to do some serious studying and write several articles each year. I was to learn that serving as a university president was, in fact, far more difficult, time-consuming, and worrisome than anything I had ever experienced."[1]

In the early 2000s, one cannot imagine such an expectation.

To accept that one may be destined for university administration is to acknowledge the primacy of intellectual inquiry and the students of inquiry—young enrollees and more mature faculty. It is to be willing to devote one's talents, time, and emotions to seeking and allocating resources and to guiding those resources in the intellectual, professional, and social development of young people and society as a whole.

To be a faculty member of a respected university is a noble calling. To be a chosen leader or administrator within the university community is a special calling. It is, at the same time, challenging, exciting, and humbling.

It is satisfying and rewarding just to be among learned faculty, as an instructor or professor. To be an administrator, to whom leadership and management are delegated by that faculty and its constituency, brings special satisfaction and reward, as well as a few frustrations. Regardless of one's experiences in universities, the number of universities one has worked in, or the number and types of prior administrative positions one has held, a new president is due many surprises. It is incumbent that one considering or being considered for a state university presidency invest considerable time in reviewing and securing one's own perspectives. The chapters that immediately follow are intended to help in that process.

CHAPTER 1

The State University
in the Twenty-first Century

The state university that you, as a new president, may lead in the first decades of the twenty-first century is considerably different from that in which you likely studied or served during early faculty years. Some presidential roles, therefore, will be different—and perhaps more challenging—than those of the presidents under whom you studied or served. In short, you will be the CEO of a multi-faceted, knowledge-oriented business that functions to a greater degree within the behaviors of a free-market economic system, even though in full or in part a "state agency" subject to state regulations and policies. Unchanged is that the institution is a valuable state entity, perceived by its people as "their institution," available to them and their families, businesses, professions, and communities as a knowledge and intellectual resource.

Here are some state university features, not absent in earlier decades, but which are, in the twenty-first century, sharply more evident and which have a greater impact on the institution and its president.

1. Intense competition for state funds. Primary and secondary education, welfare programs, prisons, economic development incentives or other gubernatorial or legislative initiatives often seem a higher priority for some of the state funds. Every state legislator has public school districts in their legislative district and a good many have a community college, both strong funding competitors.

2. Higher employment costs. Not only have salaries increased, fringe benefit costs—for health insurance, workmen's compensation, unemployment insurance, and social security—have increased far more rapidly than salaries or inflation.

3. More dependence upon student fees, donations, and grants and contracts, a consequence of the first two features. This affects program direction, management decisions and, certainly, the focus and time investment of a president.

4. A more diverse student population, faculty roster, and statewide clientele, in terms of race and ethnicity, than in earlier years. This is evident in the change in the enrollment patterns of men vs. women in specific disciplines: for example, there are far more women in engineering and veterinary medicine and more men in nursing and fashion design than previously.

5. Intense competition for students and the fees they pay, a consequence of the previous points as well as the increased awareness of students to alternative colleges and the recruitment efforts of all colleges.

6. Student preferences for apartment or other independent living arrangements, outside the purview of residence hall policies, and with more amenities than in most university facilities. Added to that is cost competition. University housing systems pay for "residence hall staffing," and private housing investors get the tax benefit of depreciation.

7. A lower proportion of tenure and tenure-track faculty resulting from increased budget dependence on short-term grants and contracts.

8. More open and aggressive student recruitment and enticement beyond state lines, including in-state tuition for certain out-of-state students, perhaps those of high ability, enrolled in unique curricula, or from nearby counties of adjacent states.

9. Differential pricing of curricula or courses, with higher fees for the more costly or higher demand programs and lower fees for those where competition for students is stronger. Pricing is a marketing strategy.

10. Finding a job for the spouse of a recruited faculty or administrator.

11. More associated businesses than just housing, intercollegiate athletics, a museum and a student union. There may well be a research park, a business "incubator" building or facility with space and services rented to start-up companies, testing laboratories, and invention licensing, as well as diagnostic services, plant or animal germ plasm sales, publishing, and/or university clinic and hospital.

12. Outsourcing of some management and service functions, such as food service, janitorial, or information systems.

13. More faculty and staff inter-relationships with the private sector, including dual employment, and potential conflicts of interest these inter-relationships bring. While there are obvious benefits to the state, and enhanced economic and social impact by the university, potential complications need to be considered, monitored, and addressed.

14. High technology costs in virtually every discipline and support unit. Whereas the library was once a "collection" of materials, it is today more of an "entree"—through costly technology—to the global collection of knowledge.

15. Pressing needs in physical infrastructure. Just as a city's first- and second-generation bridges and utility pipes have aged, so have the physical components of universities that are well along in their second century.

Although there is tremendous range in size and complexity of state universities, none is without exposure to or impact from most of the features listed in the preceding points. These affect not only the skills required and attention demanded of a president, they certainly affect the type and extent of administrative structure needed and the skills and strengths of those who assist the president in university leadership and management.

CHAPTER

The State University Presidency

Karen Hendricks of Cincinnati, Ohio, is a trustee of both The Ohio State University, a university of more than 55,000 students; a number of professional schools, including an academic health center, and five hospitals, a heavy research emphasis, and a budget exceeding $3 billion, and the Association of Governing Boards of Universities and Colleges. She has been an executive with Procter & Gamble and the Dial Corporation and CEO of Baldwin Piano & Organ. She has many bases for characterizing a state university presidency. Almost her first words in a generous phone conversation about the presidency were to call it a "daunting job, demanding an awesome array of skill sets."

Even the presidency of a smaller (not in public respect, but in breadth or budget) state university needs that "awesome array of skill sets" to deal with the many constituencies: faculty, students, alumni, governing board, governor, legislators, community and, often, statewide industry groups. Many with competing or conflicting priorities and interests.

Soon after my appointment as Kansas State's president had been announced, former Nebraska governor Frank Morrison asked me if I knew how political my job would be. I smiled and said I did. But, I had more to learn.

Since leaving the university presidency, my experiences and exposures have added to my perspective. From that, and from conversations with other presidents, trustees, and others, I offer several comparisons that I believe are cogent and that may help put the presidency in perspective. These underlie some of the discussions in later pages.

1. In terms of prerogatives, public exposure, and expected/accepted behavior, a university presidency is somewhere between that of a governor and a corporate CEO. (a) The corporate CEO needs board approval for major policy change; a governor needs legislative concurrence; a university president often needs both board

approval and faculty senate or general faculty concurrence. (b) A CEO's major personnel actions or changes in product line are generally reported only in limited circulation industry journals, if at all; a governor's personnel actions and starting/closing of programs are state-wide news; a university president's actions are state-wide news only if they involve athletics, closing or merging colleges, or a legal appeal. (c) A CEO's private life and family are rarely news; a governor's life and family are "free game"; a university president's life and family are more likely just the subjects of periodic and descriptive feature articles.

2.   As a university department head, dean, vice president, or provost, you had a supervising administrator who served as a convenient anchor—a reactor, coach, and supporter of your judgments and actions. When you become a president, except for a physically distant board, each member with his or her own business or profession to run, and your subordinate administrative team, you are "out there all alone!" In this respect, there is considerable similarity to that of a corporate CEO and a governor, as well as to a mayor, school superintendent, or a minister.

3.   In terms of choosing immediate staff—provosts, vice president, and assistants— consider the process in state and national government. A vice president or lieutenant governor (except in extremely rare cases) is chosen by the president or governor. So are their special assistants. Total loyalty to the top officer is primary. However, a president's cabinet nominees are subject to Senate confirmation. And, if a president is to get along with key members of Congress, much consideration will be given to persons they may advance for those cabinet spots. In the case of state cabinet officers, some require senate confirmation and some are independently elected; a governor's prerogatives are therefore limited. I parallel those cabinet positions, in some respects, to college deanships. College department heads and faculty play a significant role in dean selection. At the same time, for smooth and productive operation of either government or the university, cabinet officers or deans need to be an integral part of the overall management team.

4.   As with a governor, U.S. president, or corporate CEO, your presence and your words are of high symbolic value. Visibility and evidence of interest are often more important than specific decisions or actions. At this writing, President George W. Bush is making his fifth visit to hurricane damaged Louisiana and Mississippi. And, each of us listens attentively to the State of the Union or State of the State address each January to see if higher education, research, or other of our interests is mentioned. A university president's presence and words are noticed.

Because a state university presidency is such a daunting job, and is a very public position, it seems to me important that one considering a presidency have the position in some perspective, relative to other public or visible positions. My hope is that these comparisons will help with that perspective.

CHAPTER

Know Yourself—and Your Spouse

"One thing you'll need is a thick skin," I was told by a Nebraska publisher before departing for Kansas State. Two years later, on a morning jog, I was attacked by a pair of 25-pound Dalmations. They left some marks, but there was no blood!

You also need a high level of physical and emotional energy. And, you need a tolerance to the amorphous nature of university operations. Especially, you need a passion for higher education, for developing young people, for discovery, and for sharing the talents and resources of the university with the economic and social needs of the state. So, too, will your spouse.

Consider how much you have.

You need a strong ethic, a solid sense of what is right or wrong. Are you willing to "take a stand," even against compelling pressures, to express that ethic? You need to respect and feel comfortable with your own competencies and skills. You need to be one who respects, has a sincere interest in, and builds other people.

State university leadership is not a one-person job, so a president need not be the ultimate in every important trait or competency. Make a list of your strengths and a separate list of your limitations.

Ask yourself some questions. What interactions or tasks do I enjoy? What do I tend to avoid? What parts of university life and work do I like? What parts frustrate? Do I delegate well? Or, am I a "control freak?" Am I a private person? Or, am I a public personality? Can I relate to students as well as to professors? Can I relate to union members as well as to corporate executives? Can I relate to people of diverse cultures and ethnicity?

Have you given yourself the full university acquaintance and awareness that will help you in a presidency? Peter Magrath, who later became president of three universities and of the National Association of State Universities and Land

Grant Colleges (NASULGC) had been a political science major at the University of New Hampshire and, in time, dean of arts and sciences at the University of Nebraska. He was described to me at Nebraska as the first arts and sciences dean in memory to attend an outstate agricultural research field day. Such acquaintance and awareness would serve him well, not only at Nebraska; two of the state universities he would later head, Minnesota and Missouri, were in major agricultural states and had large agricultural research and extension programs.

Identify the areas where you will need colleagues with specific skills or behaviors that will complement, reinforce, or support yours. This does not suggest that you can expect to delegate all responsibility in any sector, all legislative relationships to a lobbyist, all academic leadership to a provost, or all financial matters to a vice president. You will lead—and be responsible for—the total university and its relationships, so you need to identify the areas where you will have a steep learning curve and will need especially strong and experienced people beside you.

You may have completed, in earlier years, some personality, interest, or management type tests or profiles. Review these and what they told you. Are they still valid?

Is your spouse involved and growing in his or her own professional career? How will that be influenced? What accommodations would that suggest in your presidential staffing and operations?

Is your spouse supportive and enthusiastic about university leadership? Have you discussed and do you agree on the role your spouse might play? My wife had long enjoyed the university community, had been an adviser to groups on two campuses, and had hosted student, faculty, and related groups throughout our university years.

If you have pre-college-age children, how would your assuming a presidency affect them? Would they adapt to the lifestyle and public exposure of a presidential family?

Are you willing to risk being removed from office; tenure does not apply to administrative positions. University of Nebraska – Lincoln Chancellor Harvey Perlman offered this advice: "Don't do it if you really need to do it; you have to be prepared to give the job up without any remorse at a moment's notice." Are you willing to be publicly exposed as a nominee or candidate and not be selected?

A university presidency is a noble calling. It is filled with potential for service to young people, a state's economy, and society as a whole. It can provide satisfactions many would consider unequalled, certainly numerous, generous, and sustaining. If you are equipped and prepared, and if you fit well the university you are chosen to head (next chapter), it can be fun— most days!

CHAPTER

The Institution and Its System

Dr. Elisabeth Zinser, president of Southern Oregon University since 2001, has had a remarkable career in university leadership. I visited the University of Idaho during her presidency there in the 1990s and was impressed with her leadership. Between Idaho and Oregon, she served six years as chancellor of the Lexington campus of the University of Kentucky.

Zinser's resume mentions a brief interlude as president of Gallaudet University in Washington, D.C., dedicated to deaf and hard-of-hearing students. Impressed with her credentials and her background in the health field, Gallaudet trustees chose Zinser. But hiring a hearing person collided with a growing imperative in the deaf community for empowerment, recognition, and acceptance in the full spectrum of professions and occupations. Gallaudet's presidency had become a symbol of that imperative: the trustees had passed over several hearing-impaired persons, and that triggered intense student demonstrations aimed at the trustees.

Zinser's response was to travel to Washington early to meet with key involved people. She recognized and gave voice to the situation as a meaningful turning point for the deaf community. She then resigned (within days of being named), paving the way for trustees to appoint a deaf person.

Would the university with an open presidency fit you? Would you fit that university? How would you respond if faced with a "curve ball" upon accepting the post?

Would you be comfortable in that geographic area? Could you communicate well with people of the state or the town? Do you know and understand that local or state population's ethnicity and culture?

Study the university's web site, as well as the position announcement and associated materials. Scan the city's web site and those of the community and student newspapers.

Would your discipline and your specific experiences be assets in competing for the job or functioning in the job itself? Or, would your discipline be a handicap?

To one experienced in the presidency the latter may seem an unwarranted concern. Once president, the responsibility to be fair and objective in supporting and leading all university disciplines is clearly paramount. However, discipline perceptions and biases exist in screening/selection committees and among the faculty and students they represent. Is there an apparent bias for or against a specific discipline? It is not uncommon for a university to seek a president of a discipline different from that of the departing president, for some faculty and deans to hope the board will avoid a discipline dominant in the university, or for a board to seek or an industry group to urge choosing a president from that discipline.

Soon after I had left my faculty position at Iowa State, the university was seeking a replacement for retiring President Dr. James Hilton, an animal scientist by training. An Iowa farm leader called me for some nominations, "We have to have another president from agriculture," he said.

It was evident to me that Iowa State's Academic Vice President Dr. Robert Parks, a historian, was the likely and proper choice. As dean of instruction a few years earlier, he had been very involved and supportive in some curriculum matters in our college of agriculture and I had heard him articulate very clearly the full university mission.

I could suggest a couple of well-equipped agricultural people, and did, but "Look," I said, "when a person becomes president he or she is responsible for the total university; the president does not have time to play the agriculture role. That is what the dean is for. Iowa State and Iowa agriculture would have a good person in Dr. Parks."

When Parks was appointed, I did note the media release carried a reference to his year of service in the U.S. Department of Agriculture, working on a history project. Both the Iowa Board and Parks were cognizant of the agricultural industry's concerns.

Most to the point: Have you sufficient perspective and empathy to embrace the disciplines and colleges of that university, and can you demonstrate that perspective and empathy?

Have there been some recent university events of which you should be aware? Are there some "land mines" or some "golden opportunities" these events suggest?

Having served previously in two of Nebraska's neighboring states and being dean in a third, I had watched rather closely the efforts by that state's agricultural leaders to elevate the University of Nebraska's agricultural programs to the status of a separate "campus," with its own chancellor, paralleling the University's medical campus in Omaha. Over objections of the university administration and regents, they had taken the issue to the state unicameral. The legislative result was a vice chancellor for an "Institute of Agriculture and Natural Resources" on the Lincoln campus, but reporting to both the campus chancellor and university president.

When first contacted to consider the vice chancellor's position, I declined; I feared the fight was not over and I was not about to get in the middle. In time, Lincoln campus Chancellor Jim Zumberge convinced me the fight was over, the administration and regents were happy with the result, and it would be a golden opportunity for whoever was the first vice chancellor. He was right.

The state's energized agricultural leadership, encouragement by the chancellor and president, and regent determination to support agriculture, plus legislative follow-through on the compromise it had approved, were to bring extraordinary steps in salaries, program support, and construction funds.

At the same time, there had resulted some strains and jealousies on the Lincoln campus. As a vice chancellor, I would need to do some "back-filling." I would need to spend time with other colleges and units, foster joint efforts, and encourage university-wide political support by the newly-designated Institute's clientele.

Where does the university stand in relation to other state colleges and universities in that state, in enrollment, budget, faculty strength, program breadth, and political support? Does state law allow public employees to be represented by a bargaining unit? If so, are faculty or other staff unionized? Is the university "free-standing," with its own board? Or, is it part of a multi-university board system, with a board staff coordinating and communicating policy? Or, are you considering a campus chancellorship within a multi-campus university headed by a president?

As president in a multi-university regents system, I envied my presidential friends who had their own boards. Board members in such instances, I observed, worked without reservation to strengthen their institution. They pursued with undivided focus that university's mission.

Such a circumstance would be without the periodic "in-fighting" among presidents and competition for board attention and support. It would be without evident or perceived university loyalties of board members as they debated program approvals, capital improvements, or budget requests.

Some of my friends responded, "But, at least you don't have the board telling you how to run the university or which football coach to hire!" A single-university board can be "too close" to a university's operation.

Most of my university career was in universities that were part of a multiple university system. Presidents reported directly to the board, but an executive officer or commissioner served a coordinating role. In each case, two major universities, the "University of ___" and the land-grant "_____ State University," were larger in enrollment, budget, breadth of program, and clientele base.

The exception was the University of Nebraska, operating under an elected board of regents, serving both the land grant and "University of" roles, and headed by a president. There were three campuses (now four), each headed by a chancellor. A separate state college system had its own board of regents.

California parallels the Nebraska system, with a 10-campus University of California and a separate State University system with 23 institutions.

Some states with more than one university or university system board have some form of "super board," with perhaps specific authority for approving major construction, legislative requests, or new programs. Ohio is an example.

Any system can be effective; any system can be dysfunctional. The degree of system effectiveness and the presence or absence of presidential, campus chancellor, or trustee frustration depends on the clarity of the respective roles, communication, and goodwill. Unfortunately, that is difficult to assess until you are "in the position." But learn what you can. Find a route to several people in the system and ask.

By Nebraska law, my position of vice chancellor for agriculture and natural resources reported "to the chancellor of University of Nebraska – Lincoln and the president of the University for all matters . . ." The experience was virtually without frustration; I saw the campus chancellor as my immediate guide and support, he and the president communicated well, and the president generously provided the support of his office as needed. The two were consistent in items related to my responsibility and, through them, there was clear and focused board support.

I have had fully constructive experiences (though, admittedly, some frustrations) in the other systems in which I have worked. I have watched board members and presidents play their roles, with rare exception, with mutual respect and positive behavior. My clear preference, though, based on my own experience and other presidents' apparent degree of satisfaction vs. frustration, would be for a single-university board.

Should the university be part of a multi-university board system, I would press hard for a board committee focused on my institution. If such could not be achieved, I would work especially closely with two or three board members, not necessarily alumni of my institution, but with clear empathy for my institution and its mission.

No multi-campus or multi-university system is without stress. Competition for mission, attention, resources, program approval, and dollars is ever-present. Though presidents may accept a system board's judgments, their units, faculties, or clientele may feel the university has received unfair treatment. A president often has to help them rationalize and accept the board's judgments.

If you know the university and its system and believe you can be comfortable with both, then focus your attention on the next issue, the selection process.

CHAPTER 5

The Selection Process

Before submitting credentials to a presidential screening committee or executive search firm, and certainly before an interview, talk to people you know or can find a link to—faculty, staff, alumni, or institution clientele. Get their perspectives on the institution, its promise, and its needs. Find out the names of the screening committee members and, to the extent possible, their disciplines or occupations and interests. The university website and search systems will likely yield considerable information.

If you judge that you fit that institution's characteristics and needs at this time in your life, say why in the letter you submit with your resume. Tailor that letter and the resume in accordance with what you have learned about the institution, the committee, and their emphases.

A committee will likely receive many nominations and applications; to narrow down this number to those warranting an interview is a large task. A long-time executive recruiter, who has dealt with many selection committees, observes that "it is easier for a committee to reject than to select!" To reduce a large number of qualified persons to a short list, almost any factor can be used—and may be used—to place a resumé on the reject pile.

Your discipline may be a problem for some. You may, at some point in the process, be described by a reference as aggressive, mild mannered, having been involved in a contentious issue, mostly dedicated to research, or other. If you suspect such may trigger committee concern, address that item in your letter.

Though it is not legal to discriminate against age, a committee can consider years of experience—or years remaining before normal retirement age—as a reason. If you are 35, emphasize your breadth of experience and the seasoned administrators with whom you have worked. If 60, mention indicators of vigor and health and list some things you want to accomplish in the next ten years. Let them know retirement is beyond consideration.

Screening committees comprise bright, sensitive, and discriminating people. If there is a debatable item in your resumé or letter, relative to members' perceptions of need, it will be highlighted and discussed. Anticipate that.

Most preliminary interviews with a screening committee or search firm executive, often by phone, are time limited. Make a list of the points you want to make. Because such interviews usually provide little opportunity for your questions, make any questions short and succinct, such as: What is the institution's major leadership need? What is the greatest institution opportunity in the next five years? What is the largest problem a new president will face?

A committee will have questions. What are your priorities? Undergraduate teaching? Research? Faculty salaries? Though faculty on a committee will emphasize academic credentials, Tom Lyon, former trustee and board chair of the University of Wisconsin System, says that at major research universities, the bottom line has become "Show me the money—or how you will get it!"

Write down your impressions following that interview. Get any feedback you can, from any possible source. Do the same for follow-up interviews.

For the board interview, or with a committee thereof, add to your list of questions. They will have plenty, but make sure you ask yours. If the institution is multi-campus, what are the respective roles of the institution president and campus chancellors in relating to the board? Do campus chancellors serve at the pleasure of the president? If the board is responsible for several institutions and has a board executive officer, what is that person's role? Is there a board committee focused on what would be your institution?

Does the board approve tuition rates and other fees, or do the governor and legislature get involved? Does the board get involved in athletics staff or scheduling?

How does the board articulate the university's mission? (Compare that to any printed mission that exists.) What are the board's expectations of the new president, in fund raising, curriculum leadership, administrative change, enrollment, program emphasis, new buildings, entertainment, reporting, or lobbying for state or federal funds? What is the highest or immediate priority?

Are there any current vice-presidents or other university officers who may limit a new president's effectiveness or his or her relationship with the board or the faculty?

How is the president appraised and who does it? Will the board or an evaluation committee of the board give you candid feedback, both positive and negative? Will board members provide support and help in the transition? Will they introduce you to key people?

Be prepared for more board questions, including some surprises. If you consider a question "out of bounds," have a tactful answer ready. If you do not have enough information, or if you need to consider the question more fully, say so. Do not trap yourself into a quick answer with which you will later be uncomfortable.

Suppose a board member says, "If you want my vote, you'll need to commit to close out Program X or make plans to establish a branch campus at Y, or _____." A suggested response, "Is this an item that has had full board discussion and has the board established a position?" Or, to a less demanding statement, "I appreciate your thoughts on that and would certainly look into the situation, but until I do that I wouldn't be in a position to make a commitment."

A couple of likely questions and some suggested answers:

"What salary and fringes would you expect?"

"I would expect them to be consistent with the status and breadth of the university and the tasks ahead. I'm aware of comparable positions with salaries and fringes of _____."

"Will you accept if offered?"

"If the offer is reasonable and if there are no unexpected conditions, yes." Or: "Once the terms and conditions are outlined and if they are reasonable, I would expect to."

If you are offered the job, it is clear the board has decided they want you, and they will not want to go through the process again.

Prior to the final interview, you, and other finalists, may have reviewed salary and other details with a board executive or finance officer. This is advantageous for both you and the board; it saves time in a final negotiation and helps avoid misunderstandings. Establish salary, other compensation, moving expenses, residence and entertainment expense, and travel expense (and/or any compensation) for your spouse.

Two other items may need to be discussed and settled: (1) Does your spouse seek employment within the university or an allied unit? (2) Are you qualified for and would you be granted a professorship title and academic tenure in a university department? The latter item can be especially problematic where the presidency is of a multi-campus system. It is far better to clarify such issues via appropriate interviews or reviews early than to try to arrange or negotiate later.

If any of the compensation, expense, or fringe benefit is to come from a university foundation, get assurance that it has been agreed to by foundation officers.

It is often valuable to a university for its president to serve on one or more corporate boards. Does the board concur? Will board members help bring this about? Is there a policy regarding the time and compensation for such corporate board service? Should one take leave and retain the compensation? Or, should the compensation go to the university or its foundation?

This is also the time to review any item where you feel the need for more discussion or confirmation of impressions you gained earlier. It is also the time to discuss your steps in the interval before you assume the presidential duties, and a time schedule for those steps.

When and where will the announcement of your appointment be made? Can it be on the campus? Will there be an opportunity for you to meet with key university people at that time or in the near future? Are there certain public officials you should be introduced to or that you should call on soon?

Discuss any specific reassignments in the administrative team you may want to consider. Are there any constraints on your proceeding to initiate those changes and recruit for any vacancies?

Should a term or open-ended contract be involved, make sure you are comfortable with all its features. Be sure you get your concerns and questions answered in that final board meeting or in the next few hours with the board chair. Take time; leave nothing in doubt. Be sure you are comfortable—that your expectations are the same as those of the board—before any public announcement is made.

Once that announcement is made your need for specific knowledge is even greater. Knowledge is Power! It is also comfort and confidence. The next section is devoted to that knowledge base.

PART II

The Knowledge Base

After serving as a university president, I went through the U.S. Senate confirmation process for a subcabinet presidential appointment. A nominee can expect a lot of tough questions from both senators and their staff, especially if the senate majority party is not that of the president. They will ask about the nominee's previous positions, speeches, and writings, and will have many questions about the operations of the unit one is nominated to head.

For four weeks, I studied agency budgets, programs, related legislation and, especially, recent appropriations and accompanying committee reports. Key personnel in both my future office and the agencies I was to supervise spent hours briefing me. During that process, I became well acquainted with the people who would be key members of my management team.

It struck me that if I had known the day I arrived on campus as much about the university I was to head—and the work of the people in the key spots—as I did about the agency group I was to supervise the day I was confirmed by the Senate, I would have been better equipped and more confident to begin the presidential task.

Here are some things you need to know.

CHAPTER 6

Know the Key Staff

Key staff can make or break your presidency. They can help make your job satisfying—even fun most days—and your leadership fully effective, or they can limit your effectiveness and make your life difficult and frustrating.

Whether you are promoted to a presidency from within, returning to an institution you served before, or going to a new and unfamiliar university, make a list of key staff. From the institution's web site, Google, or elsewhere, find out all you can about each person in a key position. Among the key staff: Does ethnic diversity reflect or parallel the diversity of your faculty or of the state's population? What is the proportion of women vs. men? Is there staff with experience in the private sector, federal government (agency or congressional staff), other countries, or other types of universities?

Consider the collective strengths, limitations, and voids, and how you think each person might work with you. All this should be in relation to the administrative structure that now exists or that you may consider, the charges the board gave you, and any pledges you made to the board.

Each of these key staff can be a good source of orienting information and advice, and most or all will be eager to provide that. Any that are not will be a problem.

As soon as physically possible, ask each to tell you the three biggest issues they think you will face. At the same time, ask each for a current two-page resumé plus the top three challenges they face, the top three things they have achieved or led in the past three years, what "drives them" in their life and institution work, and what they would like to be doing in five years. Have them attach copies of their last three publications, speeches, or project reports.

Emphasize to each the importance of your fully knowing and understanding each of them and the immediacy of that. To underline that, ask for the resumé and attached items within a few days of your being named.

Who should be included in this request? Include every key person who reports or relates to the president—vice presidents, provosts, deans, directors, and assistants to the president. Though in some universities deans report to or through a provost, they must be, and must consider themselves to be, major members of your administrative team.

Not only is the information you gain valuable to you; they will have ensured that you know them, their accomplishments, and what drives them.

What will you find in those resumés, challenges, publications, reports, and "driving forces?" Will there be focus on student success, recruitment, and retention? Will sensitivity to state-wide clientele and to the state's economic and societal needs and goals be evident? Will "total quality management," financial accountability, or simplifying financial processes be mentioned? Will university or college missions or directional goals be referenced? Will you see reports on budget allocation systems or on research output and impact?

Study these, and then follow up quickly with individual visits. An hour with each is likely needed to establish or confirm personal acquaintance and allow elaboration of the written materials each has given you.

The earlier these visits occur, the better! Each of those staff will have some apprehensions about how they will relate to you. Those with faculty rank will wonder if they should submit their resignations and return to faculty posts. Do not delay. The job you will be leaving will soon be handled by someone else. You are a "lame duck" already; that job can get along while you spend critical time with key staff related to your new position.

Do not let the presence of your predecessor deter you from these visits. In fact, courtesy dictates that your predecessor be your first visit.

Ask questions during these visits; fill in the blanks about experience, focus, and challenges. And, in some of those visits, ask, "Who are the most effective people among current administrators?" "Are there any whose talents suggest added or different responsibility?" "Which will be most valuable to me?"

If one of those key staff, or one of their friends, tells you that you "can't get along without them," there is 99 percent certainty that you can! Either respond with, "tell me more," or ignore it. Depending on the party who tells you that, such as a board member (very unlikely) or a key legislator, in time, you could tell the staff member, "I'm going to make a few changes, but I'd like for you to stay on for six months to help identify and train a new person."

Not to have these visits with key staff before assuming office handicaps you in management and personnel options you need to consider. It also handicaps those key staff in considering their future position security and options.

Should you be promoted to a presidency that is vacant and immediately assume office, that would affect only the timing and circumstances of those visits, not the content or need.

Personnel knowledge is a two-way street. Those key people also need to know you.

CHAPTER 7

Make Sure the Key Staff Know You

Give key staff the same package of information they are giving you. They will have tracked you on Google or your university's (or business' or agency's) website. If you are promoted to a presidency from within, or are returning to an institution you served earlier, they will know you or, at least, think they do. Make sure!

Although they may know the facts—degrees, positions, recognitions, and organization memberships—they likely will not have seen what you consider your most important publications, speeches, or reports; nor will they really know what drives you.

They need to have, directly from you, your resumé, what you consider to be your top achievements or leadership successes, your recent publications, speeches, or project reports, and, especially, what drives you in your life and institution work.

Unfortunately, the process of screening and selecting university presidents often leaves out most key staff with whom a new president may work. Unless you are being promoted from within or have previously been on the faculty, they have probably had no close contact with you.

A presidential selection process is commonly different from that used for selecting department heads and deans, where key staff are routinely involved. A typical presidential screening committee includes four to six faculty named by the faculty senate, students named by student government, and alumni named by the alumni association. It may include a dean or a vice president and, in some cases, finalists are brought to the campus for a brief tour, perhaps even a public presentation, but interaction with key staff is limited. If a search firm is involved, there would likely have been even less staff interaction with the finalists.

Key staff will probably not know the charges the board may have given you or the pledges you may have made to the board. To the extent and in the form that these can be shared, they should be, either in the written material you provide or in your individual visits with those key staff. Each key staff can then better judge if he or she will fit with what needs to be done in your administration. And, if you need to make a change, the person affected can better accept your judgment.

Next, what about the budget, the status of university programs (student enrollment and success rate, output and state impact of research and extension programs), university traditions and icons, and operating or personnel policies?

CHAPTER 8

Analyze the Budget and Budget Policy

Some presidents do not want to know about the budget; they depend on a financial vice president having knowledge of it. In doing so, they give up critical knowledge they need for informed management decisions and perhaps some of the potential impact of their presidency.

Get a summary of the current and projected income sources. Though it is a state university you will be leading, likely less than 50 percent and, for some, less than ten percent of expenditures will come from state appropriations. Of the University of Virginia's revenues in the fiscal year (FY) 2004, about seven percent came from state appropriations.[2]

More typical of major state universities without a medical school, 32 percent of Iowa State's FY '04 revenues came from state appropriations, 26 percent from grants and contracts, and 18 percent from tuition and fees (including fees from clinics, testing, and diagnostic laboratories, campus and off-campus workshops, and even 4-H membership and events).[3] The balance was largely from auxiliary enterprises and related businesses. Less than two percent came from federal formula funds for teaching, research, or extension.

Even for a smaller state university focused largely on teaching undergraduates, and with limited graduate programs, state appropriations rarely account for more than 50 percent of revenues. At Northern Michigan University, for example, the FY '04 percent was 42.6.[4]

The continuing downward trend in proportion of state funds, from 46.1 percent in FY '95 to 36.4 percent in FY '04 at Kansas State,[5] for example, has prompted some state universities and their governing boards to suggest they be released from certain state constraints and moved to a more independent "state chartered" status.

Certainly state universities have become very entrepreneurial in their operations and fund seeking. It has clearly changed administrative focus and how program judgments are made. Iowa State reported contract and grant dollar amounts ranging from $100,000 to more than $30 million coming from each of eight different cabinet level departments and three other federal agencies in FY '04. More than $12 million came from state, county, and city government agencies.

Tuition and fees have increased sharply as a proportion of the universities' annual budgets, moving up faster, in most instances, than inflation. Media reports from both board and legislative offices across the country at this writing describe a continuation of that trend.

University conferences and short courses, from postgraduate executive training programs, to fireman training, to 4-H and youth conventions are expected to be self-supporting, in many cases including the staff time formerly financed by appropriated dollars. Some are "profit centers," generating extra funds for instruction or other university programs.

State universities are in an entrepreneurial environment.

Appropriated and Central Funds

Get, in condensed form, the current operating budget of state appropriated and other "centrally controlled" funds, such as federal formula and contract/grant overhead, and how much of each source is budgeted to each college or other unit. Insist that it be condensed to less than three pages, preferably to one. Details can be in an attachment. Too much detail in a summary document prevents one from seeing and understanding the big picture.

Get a parallel summary of expenditures for the previous fiscal year. Ask for the allocation rationale: student credits, research or extension program demand, tradition, appropriation line item, or other.

Competition in state legislatures for funds is sufficiently intense, and legislators are sufficiently aware of other university fund sources, so that appropriation amounts are less related, or not related, to enrollment, authorized programs, or faculty numbers. Rather, some legislatures simply provide X dollars and leave it to the governing board and universities to find the rest from student and other fees, contracts and grants, or private funds, or adjust programs accordingly.

This entrepreneurial environment has clearly impacted university administrations' allocation rationale for centrally controlled funds. For example, Dr. Stanley Johnson, Vice Provost and Director of Extension at Iowa State University from 1996 to 2005, shifted appropriated and federal formula money *toward* those programs that had been successful in generating grant and contract funds and user fees. By doing so, he further enhanced the programs that clientele apparently considered valuable enough to pay for and that society's elected representatives has apparently placed in priority (the agencies and programs to which the political process appropriated money).

Further, this allocation rationale rewarded the staff and units that adjusted their extension education programs—in manufacturing, ISO certification, marketing, human nutrition, environment, natural resources, pest control, community development, water management, or whatever—toward what users and society had apparently placed in priority.

Not all of Extension's appropriated, formula, and overhead money at Iowa State had gone that way, and this does not suggest using such an allocation rationale in all university endeavors. This is especially so in the case of undergraduate instruction or for certain research and extension programs deemed critical to clientele but without significant external funding potential.

Instruction, academic advising, and other student-related functions are less the target of federal or state grant programs—most student-related money goes directly to students via loans and grants—but some grant programs do exist and I expect an increasing trend.

Separately Budgeted Units

Get succinct budget summaries for separately budgeted units, such as intercollegiate athletics, residence halls, research parks, or student unions, where earned or other outside income funds most or all of the expenditures.

I was surprised to learn soon after becoming president that our department of intercollegiate athletics had nearly $500,000 in negative net worth. It had three delinquent loans plus unpaid bills that extended back nearly a year. A few months later, I discovered a germ plasm sales unit with more than $200,000 in old and hardly recoverable accounts receivable.

Get from your finance officer a balance sheet (a statement of assets, liabilities, and net worth) as well as the previous year's statement of income and expenditures for each of these units. You are likely aware that the 2002 Sarbanes-Oxley legislation requires a CEO signature attesting to completeness and accuracy of corporate financial reports. That may be a good policy for your separately budgeted units. Ask each unit director to sign such a statement *and* certify that the summary includes all accounts and programs that relate in any way to their activities. More than once I have encountered separate accounts held elsewhere with either "hidden surpluses" or big deficits.

If the reports you receive raise any questions in your mind, get a fully independent audit and review.

Financial Policies and Regulations

Ask your finance officer for a summary of state policies or regulations, board policy, and institutional policies regarding expenditure authority and required processes. Ask that it cite information sources. Institutions and their units sometimes follow traditions that are different from authority or policy. It is well for staff to know the president expects adherence to regulations and written policy.

Contract/grant Overhead Funds

Find out the institution's contract and grant overhead rates and internal allocation policies for that overhead money. It is not uncommon for a university to have held and allocated most of the overhead funds to central units, such as a business office or library. However, incentive-minded administrations will have a policy that moves reasonable proportions to deans and department heads or other grant-getting units, and some to the principal investigators. Those units or individuals sought and obtained the grants or contracts, perhaps spent college or department travel money getting them, and have other overhead costs attributable to the increased work volume.

At the same time, some faculty or departments have a tendency to hoard such overhead money "for a rainy day." An associate dean recently lamented to me that one of her departments was $100,000 short in meeting salary and other costs for the fiscal year, but principal investigators in that department had more than $200,000 unspent money in their overhead accounts. My response, "You need a new policy for overhead accounts."

Former South Dakota State University President Hilton Briggs addressed that faculty hoarding tendency and a library shortfall at the same time. He instructed his finance officer to sweep up balances above a certain amount from all auxiliary accounts and transfer the money to finance library acquisitions. There was a lot of faculty, department head, and dean (including me) complaint—and a policy review and revision would have been better received—but he cured the hoarding habit.

Brainstorming with that associate dean brought out some policy options, including a ceiling on year-end balances, faculty loaning "their" overhead funds to the university with interest, and giving a department head/chairman authority to use such accumulated funds for department-wide equipment needs. Policy should encourage constructive and timely use of the money while retaining faculty and department incentive and reward.

University Foundation

Your foundation likely handles a good many accounts: private funds for university colleges, departments, other units, and perhaps individual faculty projects, as well as for your office. You and your finance officer should have access to at least annual summaries of those accounts: income, expenditures, and year-end balances. Deans should have access to that information for departments and programs in their college.

Find out who approves expenditures from such accounts. Approval of at least one supervisor—above the party that would use the funds—should be required. To not require such approval invites abuse of such funds.

A university runs on money. Know where it comes from, where it is spent, and why. You will then better know your prerogatives and flexibility in budget and program decisions.

So much for the budget and budget policy. Now, let us take a look at program and people data.

CHA**P**TER

Study the Data

My first task as a new associate dean at Kansas State, having arrived in June, was to send dismissal letters to 95 students, mostly freshmen. First, though, I studied each of those students' files—their high school grades, ACT scores, and college course loads and grades—and made a discovery. For at least a third of those 95, had I looked at the high school grades and ACT scores at university entry, I would have predicted at least a B average at the university. For another third, I would have predicted some difficulty, but probably a C average for most.

There were many examples of a student's credit load and course selection inconsistent with their ACT scores and high school grades. Too many who were average in academic ability had enrolled in 18 or more credits. Too many students scoring relatively low in quantitative skills but high in linguistic skills had started their college experience in math and chemistry instead of biology and a social science course.

Those data, though only estimates based on my personal study, gave me a basis for two management judgments: (1) we could increase enrollment by increasing retention. (2) To increase retention, we needed to budget faculty time for academic advising, and train those advisers. Both the university and future students would be winners!

To understand the current status of the university—and trends —and to exercise your management functions with confidence, you need data. Though some data will need to come from budget or other offices, an institutional research office can be a major source.

In some instances, data on trends will be the most important. Note in Tables 9.1, 9.2, and 9.3, the evident trends among faculty and students in proportions of women and men and among racial/ethnic groups in U.S. degree-granting institutions. I would want such data for my university.

Table 9.1

Percentage of Women and Men Enrolled in U.S. Degree Granting Institutions*

	1970	2001	Projected 2013
Women	41.2	56.3	57.4
Men	58.8	43.7	42.6

*Percentages calculated from National Center for Educational Statistics data. www.nces.ed.gov
Sept. 23, 2005.

Table 9.2

Percentage of Women and Men Among Instructional Faculty in U.S. Degree Granting Institutions, Fall, 2001*

	All Ranks	Professor	Assistant Professor	Instructor
Women	38.4	22.7	44.8	50.6
Men	61.6	77.3	55.2	49.4

*Percentages calculated from National Center for Educational Statistics data. www.nces.ed.gov
Sept. 23, 2005.

Table 9.3

Percentage of Professional Staff and Students by Race and Ethnicity in U.S. Degree Granting Institutions, Fall, 2001*

	Exec./Admin/ Managerial	Instr. & Res. Faculty	Instr. & Res. Assistants	Students
White, non-Hispanic	82.7	79.2	51.6	67.6
Black, non-Hispanic	9.3	5.6	3.5	11.6
Hispanic	3.6	3.3	3.0	9.8
Asian of Pacific Islander	2.4	4.9	7.8	6.4
Am. Indian/Alaska Native	0.6	0.5	0.4	1.0
Unknown	1.4	6.5	33.7	(3.5)**

*Percentages calculated from National Center for Educational Statistics data. www.nces.ed.gov
Sept. 23, 2005.
**Student datum is "non-resident aliens."

If you look at women vs. men enrollment trends, you will see significant increases in the proportion of women in Engineering, Veterinary Medicine, and Animal Science (now 65 to 70 percent women for the latter two on many campuses) and an increasing proportion of men in Fashion Design (now 17 percent

at Iowa State vs. three percent a decade ago), Nursing, and other curricula historically targeted largely by women.

Disappearance of curriculum stereotyping is long overdue, in my opinion.
Absence of any social inhibition in choosing a curriculum is an important part of
"true freedom" for students!

Data must be in a form that is useable for judgments and decision-making.
That gathered for archival purposes or to satisfy a request from a systems office or
a funding agency may or may not be in that form. And, odds are high that you
will want some data not readily available. Ask that it be gathered.

I have found that it saves time and misunderstanding if I design a table with
defined columns and rows for the institutional research or other office to complete.
That helps insure that data gathered will be in the form that allows handlers to sort
and summarize the information for management understanding and judgment.

Following are some of the data I would seek early, certainly by college and,
depending on circumstances, perhaps by department.

1. Student data

   • Enrollment trends, especially numbers of new freshmen vs. transfer students.
   • Where students come from: geography, high schools, community colleges, four-
     year institutions.
   • Race and ethnicity, perhaps compared to the state's population of college-age youth.
   • Gender trends in enrollment, including trends within certain colleges.
   • Academic abilities of new students: ACT or SAT scores, high school grade
     averages, and/or class rank.
   • Student success rates at the end of first and second term, percent dismissed or
     on academic probation, percent who voluntarily fail to return, percent who
     graduate after four, four-and-a-half, or five years.
   • Student curriculum change flow among colleges, numbers, and at what stage.
   • Enrollment trends and characteristics of continuing education students: age,
     interests, educational history.

2. Faculty and staff data

   • Full-Time Equivalent FTE, by rank, budgeted to instruction vs. academic advising
     vs. administration vs. research vs. extension education.
   • FTE, by race and ethnicity, perhaps by rank and by unit, and men vs. women.
   • FTE, by rank, on state appropriated funds vs. contract, overhead, or other funds.
   • FTE, by rank and location, at off campus units.
   • New hires vs. resignations and retirements, by rank, for recent years.

3. Operations, output, and impact data

   • Percentage of courses and/or student credits, by course level, taught by senior
     faculty, vs. junior faculty vs. graduate teaching assistants.
   • Publication rate per FTE senior and junior research faculty in a recent five-year
     period, in refereed vs. university vs. industry or user publications.
   • Any available data on citations of research publications in the scientific
     literature.
   • Patents, copyrights, and licensing arrangements.
   • Listings of technology transfer or application in the state's business, govern-
     ment, or societal sectors.

- Dollars of research support (travel, supplies, technicians, and graduate research assistants GRAs) per FTE senior research scientist.
- Dollars of support (travel, clerical staff, supplies) per FTE Extension faculty.
- Dollars of support (travel, clerical staff, supplies) per FTE Instructional faculty.

Not only do you need such data to understand the university and to make some judgments, your deans and department heads need these data for *their* management judgments. For them to get the most management satisfaction in doing so, they should get their college and department data at the same time you do.

Rest assured that if they know the president has requested the data, they will be taking a good look at it and figuring out how they can address any problems or issues about which the president or provost may inquire.

As you begin to review these data, I suggest you make three lists: (1) Areas that warrant commendation, (2) Areas that require attention by one or more of your management team (some may even require your personal attention), and (3) Areas where more or different data are needed or where you want more background information.

For each of those three categories, especially the last two, you will be writing down a series of questions to ask, such as: Why are student retention and success rates so much higher in College X than in College Y? Why the large number of resignations in College X? Why so few publications in Department Y and with such a large research budget? Why so many students transferring to the university from Community College X, and so few from Community College Y? How can we replicate in other units the apparent impact College X is having on their statewide clientele?

Data for each college or unit helps you understand the issues deans or others bring to your attention. "Let's look at the data," or "Please bring your data." is often the most productive response to an expressed concern. With the data, both you and the dean (or other party) can be "on the same page," have the same basis for considering the problem and charting the strategy to address it.

You will also want data from related units, some from annual reports or otherwise summarized. They may include:

- Foundation funds held in endowments, recent foundation receipt trends, or numbers of donors, perhaps categorized by dollar amount.
- Alumni Association membership, numbers and percentage.
- Graduation rates for student athletes, as well as recent conference rankings by sport.
- Debate and other student team competition and their recent winnings or rankings.

When you know the data, you will be more confident in your judgments. When others of your staff and faculty know that you know the data, they will be more confident in and accepting of your leadership judgments.

Data are vital, but quantitative. You also need to know the personal and human features of the university you will lead. What are the revered traditions? What or who are the icons? And, are there some "land mines" you should avoid? The next chapter addresses some of those.

CHAPTER 10

Traditions, Icons and Land Mines

Michael Gartner, owner of the Iowa Cubs baseball team and former president of NBC News, had observed universities and university presidents long before he became a member and president of the Iowa Board of Regents. He emphasized to me in a recent visit that knowing the top staff, the data, and the official university policies (see next chapter) does not tell a new president the whole story. New presidents, or deans or department heads, need to learn all they can about the university. Who are the actors? What have they done? What have been the major past battles? What are the university traditions? On what university strengths can you build?

Each university has an interesting history, including some people, buildings, or events that may represent "turning points" for the university or a certain college or department.

In addition to retiring President James McCain, at least three people at Kansas State would have been considered icons to generations of students and a good many faculty: retired dean of engineering M.A. "Cotton" Durland, retired dean of agriculture A.D. "Dad" Weber, and Student Affairs Vice President Chester "Chet" Peters. The nicknames and their daily use in reference reflected years of positive relationships and high regard. Each had "come up through the ranks," teaching and advising students, working with student organizations, and then being tapped for successive leadership posts.

Though Durland and Weber were not regularly seen on campus, their presence was felt. Peters was in the prime of leadership as Vice President, responsible for the student counseling center, residence systems, health, financial aids, club sports, and even early development of womens' intercollegiate athletics. Weber's name had been affixed to the Animal Science and Industry building earlier and, during my time, an engineering building would be named for Durland and a recreation building for Peters.

There was a fourth icon to long-time fans of mens' athletics, a former Kansas State basketball All-American, Ernie Barrett, who was, at my arrival, director of athletics. Barrett's enthusiasm for athletics and his gregarious and charming personality were clear assets and to most fans he was "Mr. K-State." But, management of the athletics business was not Barrett's strength. In time, I told him he needed to be reassigned to a different role, and we worked out a university-wide representation role as assistant to the president.

Barrett was not enthused about the change. And I had not recognized the degree to which a number of alumni, donors and, especially, sports reporters believed the cloak of Director of Athletics simply belonged on this former All-American. A "firestorm" of criticism at the action resulted. Although brief, and offset by accolades from faculty leaders and regents that K-State athletics would again be "under faculty control," and foundation trustees who were nervous about delinquent loans to athletics, it was intense.

Barrett resigned; the firestorm from friends, and perhaps pride, would not let him stay. Fortunately, however, he later returned to the university, where his All-American status and his personality could benefit the university in its representations to sports fans and others.

Could we have solved the management problem in athletics and, at the same time, avoided the interruption in Barrett's service to Kansas State? I could have named a Vice President or Assistant Vice President for Activities and moved all financial and rule abidance responsibility to that person. Would that have worked? Such are the issues a new president may face.

There may be some things one should know, but ignore. Just know "the background." On the Sunday afternoon at the end of my first week as dean at South Dakota State, my associate experiment station director, Dr. Al Musson, and his wife stopped by for what appeared to be a social visit, but he soon brought up "some history you need to know." He went on to describe in detail some events of more than a decade earlier, the hiring of one of my predecessors, conflicts among administrators, the "choosing up sides" by faculty, the firing of a popular department head by the Board of Regents (which had led to AAUP blacklisting the university for violating tenure), and eventual departure of that predecessor.

He summed up his review with, "You'll likely want to ignore all this in the actions you take, but knowing the history might help you understand some of the sensitivities and attitudes that you'll encounter, both on campus and off."

It was a valuable visit; Musson was both thoughtful and loyal in sharing that history.

If you are to head one of the state universities in Mississippi, it would be well to get a briefing on the Ayres case, which occupied the courts, the system regents, and each of the state's universities for more than a decade. It would help you understand some program and money allocations among universities in the system.

At Iowa State or Kansas State it would be as well to avoid getting into any conversation regarding the sale of the former's WOI-TV or of the latter's KKSU radio frequency. In each case, the sale ended some long-standing ownership tradition and pride and evoked a good bit of emotion. For a new president, there is no merit in getting involved.

What buildings are sacred? Many land-grant campuses have a Morrill Hall, named for the author of the 1862 Land Grant Act. Though the structure is likely far more than a century old and perhaps even condemned and abandoned, to raze it might risk a presidency. Conversely, it could be the centerpiece for a successful capital campaign (and just was at Iowa State).

On another campus, such risk—or opportunity—might be the columns of "Old Main" or even the old water tower designed and constructed by early engineering faculty and students.

Know the "people territory," to the extent you can, the family and other relationships within the university, community, and state. Those relationships may help or hinder some of the things you need to get done; your knowledge of them might determine which.

You cannot know all the relationships, but they exist—especially in a small population state or if your university is a few blocks from the state capitol. Just be alert, and do not hesitate to use those that can be helpful.

Now, on to those policy books.

CHAPTER 11

Scan the Policy Manuals

In the litigious twenty-first century environment, policy manuals and other written policies, available to all and adhered to in administrative actions, are basic to university operation. Especially in personnel matters, such policies can help avoid formal grievances and litigation or, if litigation should occur, provide bases for a strong university position.

Your familiarity with and adherence to such written policy sets the pattern for other administrators.

What are included in the term policy manuals? Faculty, staff, and student handbooks. Sections of staff or faculty union contracts. Perhaps a university catalog. There will also be university policies not contained in manuals or handbooks—letters and memos signed by your predecessor, a provost, or a vice president.

Scan the tables of contents of the policy manuals and those sections that seem most important. Ask university counsel if there are certain sections or provisions about which you should be especially aware. Ask counsel and other colleagues if there have been recent issues that exposed a void in policy documents. Ask your secretary for those recent policy statements made by your predecessor and other top officers.

As you scan these materials, consider who on your administrative team or elsewhere in the faculty or student governance structure is responsible for monitoring or handling any infractions. Do you note any voids? For example, are there university policies related to seeking diversity in student population, faculty or administrative positions, or to recruitment procedures, legislative lobbying, or appealing administrative decisions?

A word of caution: It is a rare policy manual that is up-to-date. Those printed and bound may be out of date within weeks of publication. Those most likely to be current are usually found in a personnel or affirmative action office and may be loose-leaf, with each page dated and noting the date of the page it replaced. For bound manuals, every preceding edition should have been kept on file. Find out who is responsible for that.

When there is disagreement or legal action, the university's position is extremely weak if there is no applicable policy or if there is inconsistency—either undated or unexplained—among different policy documents or successive editions of a manual. A related issue, documentation of conversations or actions involving potential personnel problems, is discussed in Chapter 52.

An item of immediate importance, should certain administrators be returning to faculty posts, is the salary adjustment policy (or precedent). A common policy is to move the person to an academic year appointment at a salary equal to their department's highest paid faculty of the same professorial rank. A sabbatical, to prepare for that return to teaching or research, may be a part of the policy. If neither a policy nor precedent exists, and you face such an issue, I suggest you negotiate the terms and declare those terms will be university policy until any replacement policy has been established.

PART III

Early Actions

O
n August 1, 2004, his first day on the job, University of Nebraska's new President, James Milliken, was in Scottsbluff, Nebraska, more than 400 miles west of his Lincoln office. All four campuses of the university are in the eastern half of the state; Milliken was within twenty miles of Wyoming. Milliken had been on the University of Nebraska staff earlier and returned after six years with the University of North Carolina system. By spending his first day in Scottsbluff, he sent several messages:

- To western Nebraskans, where the sparse population often feels disenfranchised by their unicameral's greater representation from metropolitan Omaha and Lincoln (not unlike the feelings in the Oklahoma panhandle, eastern Oregon, or west river South Dakota): that the university is paying attention to western Nebraska's needs.
- To the members of the unicameral and citizens across the state: that the university belongs to Nebraskans; it is a resource that is important and valuable not only in the cities with campuses but to the entire state.
- To all Nebraskans: your concerns matter to us and we are listening to you.
- To the university faculty and staff, to cooperating medical facilities across the state, to the ninety-three county extension offices, to branch research stations, and to four research and extension centers, one of which is at Scottsbluff: You are key members of the university community.
- To campus deans, department heads, and faculty: that the university serves the entire state, not just the campuses.

There can be important symbolism in about everything a university president does—and when he or she does it. For the day your appointment is announced, your first day on the job, your first week, and your first month, consider carefully the messages you want to convey and when, where, and how you want to convey them. Plan those first days very carefully.

A more common agenda for a president's first day on the job might be a - get-acquainted breakfast with faculty leadership, a mid-morning session with media, lunch in a residence hall with student leadership, perhaps an electronic greeting to field staff, and a late afternoon meeting with the local Chamber of Commerce board.

Unless there is some university problem that requires immediate input and discussion by a deans' council or other staff advisory council, avoid such meetings until you have had time to interact and work with most of the members. I had such meetings, with deans and vice presidents my first day and with a broader "consultative council" my third day, and they were probably the least productive meetings of my eleven years in the presidency.

Except for a couple persons with whom I had been long acquainted, no one was about to risk expressing herself of himself on any issue or respond to any question I asked. They were simply being cautious; they did not know how that new person in the Chair would react to whatever they might say. Both they and I needed the interaction that time and daily issues would provide before there might be free and open exchange in council meetings.

You will have some unexpected demands on your time those first days and weeks. You may get a call to meet with governor's cabinet. A board member or major donor may stop in to visit. Save some open time; do not over-schedule.

You will also have many invitations, some described as urgent and they may be high or low on your priority. Stick to your plan. Do not let those first important days get frittered away on things you can do as well and as beneficially to your leadership task a few weeks later.

Let us return to the appointment announcement, a topic mentioned first in Chapter 5, The Selection Process. Have a few words carefully prepared, for that announcement and/or for your early introduction, preferably on the campus. I suggest they include:

- Your respect for the university, its mission, faculty, and student body.
- A word on campus appearance and attractiveness.
- Your appreciation to the screening committee and the board.
- Compliments to your predecessor.
- Your philosophy of participatory leadership.
- Perhaps your intent to consider the administrative structure.

Make no commitments in those comments except your dedication to the future of the university and its mission.

James Milliken knew Nebraska and the university well, and he knew the symbolisms that would be most effective. A new president's early actions have far more significance and impact than comparable actions at a later time. That is the reason for this special section and the several chapters herein.

CHAPTER

Communicate Your Vision

Websites illustrate the almost universal attention paid by state universities and their governing boards to statements of institutional mission. Some make explicit, or rather clearly imply, differentiation from the missions of other of the state's universities. Note the following mission statement excerpts:

- Eastern Washington University: ". . . student-oriented, regionally-based, comprehensive university . . . to prepare broadly educated, technologically proficient . . . citizens."
- University of Northern Colorado: ". . . comprehensive baccalaureate and specialized graduate research university with selective admission standards . . . masters and doctoral degrees primarily in the field of education."
- Prairie View (Texas) A&M University: ". . . a state-assisted institution . . . serving a diverse ethnic and socioeconomic population . . .", and it lists a series of careers for which undergraduates are prepared.

Compare these mission statements with the following, each for a state university comprehensive in disciplines, degrees, and geographic service:

- The Ohio State University: To attain international distinction in education, scholarship, and public service.
- University of Arizona: To educate, serve, and inspire.
- University of California–Berkeley: Teaching, research, and public service.

A few mission statements that I will not cite extend to a page or more. Perhaps they were put together by committees, whose members each wanted to be sure their activity was mentioned. Such are of little value.

If a mission statement exists for your university, you likely have reviewed and discussed it with the governing board. There may be an accompanying strategic plan with specific goals and objectives. You are especially fortunate if both exist, if there is clarity in both, if there is full support by your board, and if faculty had been sufficiently involved in the process of acceptance and agreement. If such do not exist, you have both a task and a golden opportunity—to lead in their development and their approval by the board. Chapter 16, Set Goals, may be of help.

If the university's mission statement is the length of a short sermon, you have the opportunity to "interpret" it in meaningful succinctness. Regardless, with perhaps a mission statement or clear mission understanding as a base, you need to establish *your future vision* of this university—what you want it to be and how you want it to be seen at some future time, perhaps in ten years, at your retirement, or at your intended departure X years hence.

If your institution is the state's major comprehensive university—or one of two or more—in what way will you expect to have enhanced its differentiation from and status relative to the major comprehensive universities of other states? If your institution is a regional university or specialized in its disciplines, geographic focus, or primary ethnic audience, in what way will you expect to have enhanced its prominence and stature within the state and relative to peer institutions in other states?

Do you want it to be and be seen as:

- An internationally focused university in all curriculums and continuing education?
- The university most focused on the state's economic growth, in curriculum offerings, student placement, research programs, and extension education?
- The regional university most focused and effective in serving its geographic or ethnic population, both in curricula and in continuing education?
- Primarily an upper class and graduate university, with major research programs in virtually every discipline?
- The university that is —?

These visions can be inclusive of curricula and disciplines, and there is no implied exclusion of athletics or any other student, alumni, or client interest.

Some state universities or campuses within a multi-campus university are more focused in their mission. Several states, for example, have a School of Mines or a campus devoted to technology or the health sciences. For such, an appropriate vision may be:

- The supreme engineering and physical sciences university of the region. Or
- The region's supreme university in the health and biological sciences?

You need to establish and articulate *your vision* for the university and, at the same time, devote attention to the key factors in fulfilling that vision—the topics of the following chapters, particularly the next four.

Can you mold the *university's mission* and *your vision* into the many talks you will make to faculty, students, alumni, and others, especially during your first months in office? If you can, in a message that is inclusive in its attention to and respect for students and faculty, academics and athletics, technology and the arts, research and the quality of teaching, and campus focus plus statewide service, you will capture many friends for yourself and the university.

Crafting that message—inclusive, succinct, visionary, and in line with the university's stated or understood mission—deserves investment of quality time. Unless you are an especially talented communicator, find one to help craft your comments.

CHAPTER 13

Consider Your Administrative Structure

Nelson Galle, a regent for the six-university Kansas system, refers to a state university president as CEO (Chief Executive Officer) with need for three close associates: a COO (Chief Operating Officer, probably with the title of provost), a CFO (Chief Financial Officer), and a CMO (Chief Marketing Officer). His reasoning lies in the premise that a state university operates in a free market, with clients and customers that may choose any vendor, seeking funds from sources that have competitive use for dollars, and competing with other providers on product quality and price. A university, to thrive, must market aggressively, control costs, and produce high quality product in sufficient volume to achieve competitive efficiency.

Galle has been the top officer of a major corporation and more recently owned and served as CEO of a mid-sized company, but he has high empathy for the university. He and his wife have been extremely close to their alma mater, Kansas State. He has chaired alumni and foundation boards, his three children are graduates of the university, and his wife has chaired the 4-H Foundation and served on other advisory groups to the university.

The CEO and parallel acronyms may seem antithetical to those steeped in academic traditions, but the CEO and CFO acronyms are being used in some universities and the concept should not be dismissed. Rather, based on the reality of state university and society circumstance, it should, in my opinion, be considered.

Most state and private universities have a provost to whom program leadership is largely delegated. Such a position became almost universal in U.S. higher education during the last half of the twentieth century. As universities grew in size and program breadth, tasks descending on the president became so large that some major presidential duties had to be delegated. On some campuses, this delegation is rather complete, with the president considered "Mr. Outside" and the provost "Mr. Inside."

In earlier years, with smaller institutions and fewer public duties requiring presidential time, presidents were expected to have large influence on faculty selection and the academic program. Prime examples are Woodrow Wilson at Princeton and Maynard Hutchins at Chicago. Milton Eisenhower, chosen to lead Kansas State in 1943, chaired the university curriculum committee.

Whether or not one agrees with the program changes that these or other presidents brought about, such direct involvement allows the use of the skills and experiences for which a president was chosen and the perceptions gained from off-campus relationships to directly impact curriculum content and faculty building.

Although major program delegation to a provost is common and accepted as normal, a president should devote quality time to and exert constructive influence on the academic program and faculty. Further, you, as president, cannot afford to abdicate direct communication and relationships with college deans. Nor should deans be without that direct communication. Collectively, deans are—and want to be—key members of a president's administrative team. In their respective areas, they are the program leaders and the communication links with department heads and faculty.

At the same time, both you, as president, and deans must respect and adhere to the delegated responsibility of a provost or vice president for finance. For that delegated responsibility to be meaningful, and to prevent deans' concerns from unduly burying you, the provost and finance vice president need to be involved in all issues of major direction and commitment.

Whether enrolling 10,000 students or 50,000, whether expenditures are less than $100 million or well over $1 billion, and whether the university is urban or in a rural setting, a state university's programs extend beyond the campus. Staff time and dollar volume of activity in statewide research, technology transfer, extension, or continuing education may exceed, in some disciplines or sectors, the campus instructional program. The provost's program role is university-wide, and acquaintance beyond the campus *per se* is critical.

On the retirement of my vice president for academic affairs, who played a campus-focused role, his replacement was given the broader title of provost, and he and I spent one of his first days visiting two county extension offices, including an evening meeting with a county extension council. And, the provost visited a couple of branch research stations in his first months on the job. In a large university, vice provosts for instruction, research, and extension/continuing education are common.

A strong and well-prepared vice-president for finance (equivalent to the post of CFO) is a must in a large university. Multiple income sources, accountability requirements, construction, plant maintenance, and the financial aspects of university-related businesses, often including joint ventures with the private sector, require breadth of understanding and expertise. Experience in a federal or state agency, as well as in a university, and a graduate degree in accounting or business management are a help.

As I visit with university department heads and deans, I hear both complaints and praise regarding those sectors for which a CFO is responsible. Complaints focus on undue procedures, gate-keepers (those who seem to hunt for ways to stop the process), and delays. Praise goes to those who "make things happen."

Recently, a dean conveyed high praise for her university CFO who had worked for more than a year, "turning over every rock" to find money for a costly facility that was critical to a major department's long-term program. Such a CFO is a major asset to a president.

Galle's suggestion of a chief marketing officer (CMO) is based on the premise that, although the president carries a major role in relating to a university's many publics, the job is so large and so broad that full-time attention by one who lives, thinks, and functions in a marketing mode is needed. (The formal title in the private sector may be vice president for marketing, but vice president for advancement is a more logical and a more commonly used title in universities.)

What relationships or units might be led and coordinated by the CMO? They may include the state legislature, alumni association, university foundation, individual major donors, congressional delegation, state or federal agencies, student recruitment and admission, student financial aid, and intercollegiate athletics. Each of these relationships is a key marketing opportunity. The CMO would exist to see that every opportunity is pursued and effective marketing happens.

A president certainly cannot abdicate all marketing functions to a CMO, but such an officer—especially one whose personal qualities and speaking skills make him or her an attractive representative of the administration—can allow you, as president, to play a more balanced role on behalf of the total university functions.

Whether or not this CEO–COO–CFO–CMO system is appropriate for a specific university is up to the president, the board, and others to decide. The important point is that the roles—financial leadership, marketing leadership, and program leadership—are highlighted and accommodated in the administrative structure.

In a smaller university, the president may need but a senior vice president, a director of finance, and a few other central top officers and work more directly with deans. Or, a president may want a flatter organization, with separate vice presidents or directors for finance, facilities, academic programs, public affairs, and student affairs. These titles are historically more common.

Among points and suggestions that I offer, most also made by trustees, presidents, provosts, and deans, are the following:

1. You, as president, must save considerable time for planning and strategy. If too many people report directly to the president, or, if those that do, take all problems to the president, there is little time for planning and strategy.
2. Keep the structure simple, with few administrative levels between faculty and the president. Scan websites of comparable universities to study their structures. Consider options. In the offices at each level, department head, dean, and president/provost, there should be sufficient agreement on mission and priorities and sufficient communication within each office that most issues can be handled by any *one* of the persons at that level. As a dean, with associates for instruction, research, and extension, each with travel schedules, any one of the four could approve department travel requests, purchase requisitions, and appointments to classified positions. File copies were then routed among the four so all were informed.

3. Mesh student affairs with instruction and academic advising, especially for undergraduate students. Too often, I have seen a "disconnect" between academic leadership and student affairs. In selecting a new vice-president for student affairs, I involved my provost and we affixed a second title, vice-provost. However, a more logical arrangement would be a single position, vice-provost for instruction and student affairs. Instruction, academic advising, the counseling center, residence staff, and intramurals all focus on the student. Through that vice-provost can be fostered close working relationships among college academic advisers, "learning communities" in housing, and leadership development, all focused on student success and retention.

4. Consider where university-wide Extension/Continuing Education leadership should reside. This is especially significant to universities with legal responsibility for the Cooperative Extension Service (CES), but of consequence in any university with extension-type programs in multiple disciplines. A survey[6] in 2000 of the 1862 land grant universities indicated that in thirty of those responding, the CES directorship was in the agricultural college. In nineteen, the CES director was separate from the college and, in ten of those cases, carried the title of or was located in the office of vice provost or vice president. Though tradition and political influence need to be considered, society's need for extension education/technology transfer in diverse disciplines where the university holds valuable talent strongly suggests a vice provost position.

5. Integrate and coordinate instruction, research, and extension/continuing education at the college and department levels, as well as at the provost/president level. The basic structure is for each dean and department head to be responsible for instruction, research, and extension/continuing education in their disciplines. They may have associate deans and associate department heads as "program coordinators/leaders" for instruction, research, and extension. Such is a basic concept of the land-grant university, but it should not be unique to them. Education, on campus or off, will benefit. To paraphrase, "Those who write the pages in Mother Nature's Book of Knowledge may also read and interpret the pages."

6. Take advantage of the experience and wisdom of a trusted adviser, perhaps a president you served under or who has helped advance your career. Share the circumstance you face and perhaps the team building that is discussed in the next chapter. Seek their advice or their reaction to your initial judgment and plans. It can be helpful.

To summarize:

1. Organize to manage program production and output, finance, and marketing;
2. Save some presidential time to plan and strategize;
3. Keep the structure simple, with few layers;
4. Integrate instruction, research, and extension at each administrative level; and
5. Let structure be influenced by the university's unique features and tasks.

CHAPTER 14

Get the Right People on Your Team

The best book I have read with useful application to a new university presidency is *Good to Great* by Jim Collins.[7] It summarizes an exhaustive study of 12 pairs of corporations and their CEOs. Both members of each pair, at the beginning of the time period studied, were considered good. One of each pair moved over time to a defined "greatness," and the other remained "good" or faltered.

Do not be turned off because the cited book is a study of corporate leadership. Whether you are interested in a presidency, are a nominee, are in the interview process, or are a newly named president, get this book and read it. Overshadowing all other valuable messages from this study is the admonition, "Build your team first!"

Prior to the announcement of my appointment to what would be my first administrative job, while faculty were yet speculating on who would be named, one who felt he deserved promotion to the post sought me out to say that if he were not named by the dean he would fight it. I only listened, of course, but related the conversation to the dean and suggested the person be transferred to another unit before my appointment was announced. He would be happier and I would be better off short one position than to have the unhappiness in my unit. The dean obliged, transferred him to another unit, and delayed the announcement of my appointment by several weeks. My relationship with that person remained positive and warm. Rarely would a board be in a position to or want to make such an accommodation prior to the appointment of a president but, if circumstances warrant, it is worthy of discussion with the board.

The information exchange outlined in Chapters 6 and 7 is a major first step in building your team. The second step is to not assume—nor should current staff assume—that each incumbent is locked in their administrative position, their title, or their current portfolio of responsibilities.

I do not suggest an automatic "fruit basket upset" or "house cleaning." I do, however, underline that you have both opportunity and responsibility to establish *your team*. This is an item you will have discussed—or certainly should have discussed—with the board while being hired.

You should seek for your team one or more experienced incumbents who can transfer their loyalty and also provide the continuity that is helpful to faculty and staff security. One or more current administrator may request a return to teaching, research, or other previous role. On my first day as dean at South Dakota State University, Dr. Lloyd Glover, head of my Economics Department, brought me a list of ten items his department needed. Number 10 on his list was "A new department head." Glover wanted to return to his first love, teaching.

University of Texas' former President Peter Flawn[8] suggests that "any vice president you might want to keep will submit his or her resignation letter." You can refuse those.

There may be one or more top officers with whom you believe you cannot establish a good working relationship, whose goals and philosophies do not mesh with yours, or who is not getting the job done. One may carry some scars from dealings with the board, deans, or faculty, or may have been delegated more authority or responsibility than you want to delegate—and not want to give it up. There may be a void in the current team's collective skills. *Some* change is likely in order. Do not flinch.

Our country's second president, John Adams, retained George Washington's full cabinet and he and his presidency suffered severely.[9] In contrast, when George H. W. Bush was elected as successor to Ronald Reagan, though they were of the same political party, the message went to all political appointees, "There may be job for you in the new administration but, if there is, it will not likely be the same job." All were expected to submit their resignations in concert with the end of Reagan's term.

An important person is the senior secretary or administrative assistant to the president. Although likely having great respect and affection for your predecessor, the odds are high that the person has no personal agenda and can transfer total loyalty to you. That person knows the key people, their motivations, their strengths, and their foibles, and so can help you avoid some land mines. That person may be your most valuable asset in your early days in the job.

If you believe a change in a key position is needed and a resignation has not been offered, *proceed* with considered steps to bring about the change. For your leadership to be effective and satisfying, thirty minutes or an hour of awkward or difficult conversation, and perhaps negotiation on a new role, is better for you *and for the other party* than a year—or several years—of frustration!

The first weeks after being named or assuming the presidency is generally a "honeymoon;" any criticism of a new president's decisions is muted. However, that honeymoon does not last long. Do not delay!

Equally important to making the necessary changes is how and when they are made. Especially in colleges and universities, persons in high-level posts are high-ability and proud people. It is best for all parties if the resigning person makes the announcement *well before you assume the presidency* and before you make any statement regarding personnel or organization. A change then can be "without prejudice," with no suggestion of inadequate performance or schism between you and the departing person.

If you need to initiate the change, the rationale you present can help or hinder that person's self-respect, subsequent relationship with you, and productivity. You may plan to delete the position, change its duties, or combine it with another. Or, the years immediately ahead may require someone with different experiences and skills.

Openly discuss options for the person's new assignment. The information you have received, suggested in Chapter 6, Know the Key Staff, likely gave you clues to those options. Depending on his or her skills, you might move the person to head a new and challenging initiative. A tenured person can, of course, return to his or her department, though there will be budget and other implications to consider with the dean and department head.

There could be an angry reaction to a reassignment. If you anticipate that, it is helpful and reassuring to have had input from others who also see the need for change. In your visit with the person, in such a case, give a rather short deadline for an announcement by that person and have a statement of your own—including your decision to delete or change the position—ready to go.

Don't flinch and don't delay!

The next step is filling any holes. This is also the time to further consider to what extent racial or ethnic diversity or proportion of women and men should influence the recruitment and selection process and its result. Bear in mind that, where there has been a paucity of women or minorities in the university's administrative team, such a new selectee may receive more than normal scrutiny. As with any personnel selection, be sure that the person chosen is the right one for the job, that the person is equipped to succeed, and that he or she will have the colleague support needed for success.

Have board concurrence that you can begin recruitment before assuming the presidency. Again, do not delay the process if you know what you want the job or jobs to cover and the traits you want in the people you are recruiting. If you are undecided on the exact role of a specific position, or time does not allow the full consideration you want, either carry that role yourself for the immediate future, with support staff handling the details, or name an acting person.

You may have the right person internally, but are not certain how he or she would perform. Do not hesitate to appoint a person on an acting or interim basis. If it is a position in your office, "special assistant" is an alternate to "Assistant to the President." If the person does well, you can remove the interim, acting, or special handle. If not, or if the person simply does not want to continue in that position, he or she can return to a previous position without embarrassment.

You may have one or more persons in mind, a former colleague, one whom you have observed in another institution, and/or a current or former staff member at this university. Just be sure that you—and any screening committee you use—devote the time and do the checking that needs to be done to get the right person.

Current privacy laws and risk of legal action make it difficult for references, especially supervisors, to share in letters or phone visits any negative features or cautions regarding a candidate. Except for those with whom I was rather well acquainted before hiring, my best hires, by far, in universities, government, or the private sector have resulted from visiting (often accompanied by a colleague or screening committee chair) finalists, their co-workers, and others on their campuses or in their places of business. In every case, positive reinforcements and assessments or problems and concerns emerged which would not show up in a resume, letters of reference, or a traditional job interview.

When the final hiring decision was made, it was with a much higher level of confidence. I can recall no instance where the person hired after such a visit did not perform in a superb manner.

You will build your first team at this university only once. Get the right people on that team.

And, spend some time taking stock of your many constituencies.

CHAPTER

Take Stock of Your Constituencies

Several trustees (among those mentioned in the Acknowledgments section), in responding to my request for content suggestions for this book, made the point that a presidency is far more than a "super provost" position. Though a provost position is a common step to a presidency (about 28 percent of current men presidents and 46 percent of current women presidents, according to a recent survey[10]), a provost's focus is generally within the university, working with deans, department heads, faculty, students, teaching, research, and related units and programs. A president works with many constituencies beyond the university—the governing board, governor, legislators, alumni, donors, athletics supporters, parents, state industry and professional organizations, and the local business and residential community. Complaints—and support—can come from every quarter.

Several trustees also emphasized that one of the first tasks of a new president is to take stock of these external constituencies and their concerns. What do they want from the university and from your leadership? Who and how strong are the constituencies' leaders? Do they want to help? In what way can they be of most help? University constituents are like your neighbors; most want to help and are pleased when asked.

Several trustees also emphasized, "Take stock yourself! Do not depend on others to tell you about them." Early in my presidency, I spent a day with one of my senior staff in visits he arranged to "key people" in the state. All of our hosts were gracious, highly respected people with earned influence—and that influence would be of help—but I soon realized most were my colleague's old friends from earlier battles. I did not hear needs, concerns, or expectations. I needed interaction with current legislators, parents of current students, current leaders of the alumni association, leaders of diverse and potential clientele groups (socio-economic and racial/ethnic) and current leaders of industry groups.

I also needed no one between them and me. People are too reticent to candidly discuss a university's needs, shortfalls, or problems in the presence of long-time staff. They fear embarrassing one who might have been associated with, responsible for, or tolerant of those problems. They will be candid with a new president. Subsequently, in most cases I would go alone; in others I would ask an alumnus or other local person, someone with whom they would feel comfortable, to arrange a visit.

As important as what you learn is the fact that you came to listen. Constituents want to meet the new leader. They are complimented by your presence. They have things they want to say and suggestions they want to make. And, they will have some questions. They will particularly want you to know that they are eager to support and be of help. At the same time, they will want to hear your passion for higher education, your respect for "their" university, and what you have in mind for it.

Some athletic fans will want a pledge that you will take all the teams to conference championships. In my case, with the football program on probation and the athletic department's finances in a deep hole, my first expressed goals had to be (1) follow the rules and (2) balance the budget—financial management. Then I would follow with a Goal Number 3, "top half of the conference in all sports in which we compete, and a competitor for the conference championship in two or three."

These interactions are also a good time to pose a question or to outline a major problem and ask for advice. It may be space needs, enrollment, building priorities, athletics, or whatever. Responses may give you some base for your actions and judgments, and even the odds for achieving a solution.

One may receive a lot of complaints and, although new to the presidency, you may feel the need to "rise to the defense." I have found that it is well to at least include, "Tell me more." Eventually, if one listens long enough, the complainer will have fully analyzed the problem, recognized the limitations you might face in solving it, and offered their help. If they do not, ask "What do you suggest?"

Who should be on a new president's constituencies list and which are the priorities? In my book, the governor is Number 1; the governor recommends the budget to the legislature. The board chair may have and should have taken you to meet the governor, but I would arrange another visit soon. During the first months in the job, I would go see legislative leaders of both political parties and chairs of appropriations committees or sub-committees. Ask each dean and also department heads with statewide industry or professional linkages to suggest people you should get to know.

The alumni and foundation boards will have you on their first meeting agenda—and you may be ex officio on their boards. The local chamber of commerce and maybe the city council or chamber of commerce will invite you to their next board meeting. You should accept. As you meet with these leadership groups, observe the membership. Is there racial/ethnic diversity that reflects the state's citizenry? Are there "big thinkers?" Are there any large voids in the membership or the interests expressed? One should not overlook potential clientele groups, such as state associations of retailers, small businesses, manufacturers, education groups, or racial/ethnic and socio-economic groups. Certain of these groups, or individuals, you may need to seek out. It will not only give you a more complete inventory of your state's education and service needs, it can broaden the base of your university's—and your—political support.

You will be invited to each college dean's external advisory committee meeting. Those interactions can be helpful, but you should expect some lobbying. In most, you will likely hear that your predecessor did not pay enough attention to that college, and that accreditation is in jeopardy because of low-paid faculty and the need for new facilities. After the meeting, though, a very thoughtful member of the committee will seek you out to say he or she and the committee really appreciate the tasks you face and that you can count on them for any support you need.

Especially, one should not overlook the obvious—your students. Early sessions with the student senate, perhaps a couple of the college student councils, and the editorial board of the student newspaper will be helpful and pay dividends.

In order to accomplish some internal changes that you see as necessary, you may need to take along some key staff to hear the complaints themselves. Early in my presidency, I asked our alumni association to arrange a series of citizen forums across the state where I could hear, in addition to what I received from established groups, expectations and concerns about the university. Topics ranged from extension programs to athletics, but the most vividly expressed concern by parents, *in every session*, was the difficulty their son or daughter had in understanding graduate teaching assistants (GTAs) from other countries.

Back on campus, my academic vice president, John Chalmers, long pressed by budget limitations for teaching staff and accepting foreign-born GTAs as a necessary "given" in what we call research universities, had some difficulty believing and accepting this complaint. For the next forum, I took Chalmers or a dean with me. They needed to hear it directly.

After those next forums, we established a campus policy that every teaching assistant for whom English was not their first language would audition before a three-person committee, generally composed of a student, an assistant or associate dean, and a faculty member. The committee would have authority to approve the GTA for teaching, prescribe corrective training and a second audition, or insist on reassignment. A few department heads still objected, "What if I committed to a teaching assistantship when the student applied for graduate study?" Our response, "You took a risk; transfer the person to a research assistantship; move one who can be understood from research to the GTA."

By no means should a new president accept at face value every suggestion or complaint. In the case of the foreign GTAs, for example, I believe, and I shared that belief with parents, that a valuable part of the university experience is to become acquainted with people of other cultures and with other languages, which includes careful listening to their speech cadence and accents, and to work to achieve true interaction. Parents would agree to that. But a line must be drawn, a judgment made.

The second most common expression by participants in these citizen forums was "Don't try to be all things to all people." Kansas State should do those things that it can do best. Kansas has other universities and other agencies with good programs and skills.

From such visits with constituencies, you not only *learn*, but you develop an informal cadre of friends who can be counted on for advice and feedback and support!

CHAPTER

Set Goals

During the 1990s, while Eastern Europe was yet in or just emerging from the stagnation of the Soviet system and Southeast Asia was virtually exploding in technology and economic growth, I spent considerable time in universities, research institutes, and government agencies in both regions. Entrance lobbies and conference room walls in Eastern Europe featured photos and tributes to their founders. In contrast, those in Southeast Asia featured goals and objectives for the years ahead. The contrast was also evident as we concluded our program discussions. In Eastern Europe we toasted the founders; in East Asia we drank to the future.

A well-crafted mission statement and challenging, directional goals can both guide and inspire a total organization: management team, units, and individual staff. Goals convey to all that the organization, whether it is a private business, government agency, or university, is looking forward, with specific things to accomplish.

A basic human motivation is to serve a clear and understood need. If the goals of a university, college, or department are clear and have meaning to faculty and staff, each person will consider how their talents and facilities can contribute most to achieving them. Each wants some of the reward—largely satisfaction.

One goal may be to reach the top 10 percent among peer universities in student success rate. Such would bring greater attention by deans and department heads to training of academic advisers, assigning faculty time to the function, random monitoring of the performance (such as the degree to which freshman credit loads relate to high school grade average or ACT/SAT scores), and recognition of effective advisers. And, the university office of institutional research would be gathering and providing data on student persistence.

Another goal may be to reach the top twenty-five percent of peer universities in contract and grant funding. A grant-writing workshop will develop, perhaps in a research vice-provost's office, travel money to Washington will be allotted, and deans and department heads will monitor progress and reward faculty who win those grants and contracts.

Such goals for the university as well as for university units may already exist, as part of a university-wide strategic plan. If so, review that plan. As one develops or reviews goals, note how many focus on *input* (such as grant and contract dollars). How many relate to *output* (such as student retention or numbers of publications)? And how many relate to *impact*—placement or salaries of graduates, or impact on the economy of the state, an industry, government, families, or other of the state's societal or economic sectors? To the extent that existing goals fail to cover output and impact, such goals should be added.

It is the *output:* student success, dissemination of research outcomes, or effective extension programs, and the *impact:* implementation of the conveyed technology and concepts, that provide the payoff for a university's clientele. It is from the outcome and impact that the university's publics (students, their parents, other clientele, and funders) make judgments on the usefulness and value of the state university! Further, the extent to which these goals are measurable will determine how accurately the president, the management team, and others can assess progress and gain full satisfaction from that progress.

It is also important, and obvious, that the foci of many of the instruction, research, and extension goals should be on the major economic and social features and needs *of the state.* What are some of those features and future needs? Energy? Water? Transportation systems? New technology? Outmoded manufacturing? Numbers and training of primary and secondary teachers or health professionals? Government efficiencies?

I offer an example: Few issues are as critical to sustained United States' or a state's economic activity and quality of life as energy security. Escalating consumption, heavy dependence on imported oil, and competition by the exploding economies of the two billion people in India and China for both current supply and global reserves of oil mean the United States is in a precarious position. United States' energy security is dependent on global political stability, use efficiency, brakes on consumption, political judgments (such as where drilling is allowed), technology for releasing petroleum from sands and rock, and/or more renewable energy.

At this writing, I devote about a fourth of my time to renewable energy, the degree to which U. S. agriculture (broad definition, including public and private forestry, the horticultural industry, and commodity processors) and the land it manages can provide consumable energy. Our vision is that by 2025, this defined sector can provide 25 percent of the country's consumable energy. For this to occur, going from about six quads (quadrillion BTU) of renewable energy annually to more than 27 quads would require research and education in dozens of disciplines. The FY '06 federal research and development budget totals $132 billion, and much of that is for energy-related research and education to be funded by DOE and other agencies.[11] Almost every state university has one or more departments with capability that would warrant funding.

Should some of the university-wide or college goals in the university's strategic plan focus on components of energy security? Or water, transportation, training of teachers and health professionals, manufacturing, government efficiencies, or other state/national priorities? Such programs may influence how useful the university is perceived to be.

Clear goals may not only guide and inspire faculty; they may cause a donor, governor, or legislative appropriations committee to help the university achieve the goal. That is especially so if those goals relate to the societal and economic goals *of the state*.

Early in my time as dean at South Dakota State University (SDSU) a young state budget officer told me our research appropriations had remained flat because the joint House/Senate appropriations committee members wondered if our research was focused on the future. He urged me to set some clear, written goals.

Before the next legislative session, we established ten research goals, and pledged that 70 percent of our base budget and all of the 'new program' money we sought would be allocated to the ten. The first goal was to move the far edge of the Corn Belt north and west (where lower rainfall and shorter growing season limit yields). Agriculture was the state's major industry and corn was the highest value crop. It also had the largest potential for yield increase, to use more sun, water, and soil nutrients to produce more carbohydrate and protein. The next nine, in priority according to need and potential, were similarly directional and measurable.

A few minutes after our presentation to the appropriations committee the following February, a member stepped out in the hall to tell me, "Since you seem to know where your research is headed, we're going to help you get there!" All new program funds we had requested, plus inflation increases on the base budget, were provided.

Did department heads and research faculty receive the goal signal and respond? Certainly; they wanted part of that money, as well as the satisfaction of helping reach the goal! Department allocations and staff effort shifted increasingly to genetic tolerance to drought and seed tolerance to cold soil temperature, earlier maturity (allowing harvest ahead of frost), reduced insect damage to roots (that diminished absorption of moisture and nutrients), and tillage practices that conserved soil moisture.

Was there long-term impact? Near the end of my time as USDA assistant secretary, I returned to SDSU to help dedicate a new plant science building. In preparing for my dedicatory comments, I asked for current corn acreage and yield data, by county. Whereas significant corn production had earlier been limited to southeastern South Dakota, corn acreage in the central and north central regions had increased 58 and 64 percent, respectively. The far edge of the Corn Belt had moved at least 100 miles north and west.

If a featured university goal is to prepare graduates to compete and live in a global society, curriculum committees and advisers will consider requiring or recommending foreign languages and courses in foreign cultures. Some instructors will refine their course outlines. An economics instructor may devote more time to exchange rates, diverse economic systems, and influences on global supply and demand. Friedman's *The World is Flat*[12] may become required reading.

The global incidence of iron deficiency, anemia, and Vitamin A deficiencies, almost endemic in less developed countries, may be discussed in a nutrition course. The Engineering College may add a seminar on global engineering issues, or add to certain courses the ethics of contracting or professional licensing in example countries.

If a companion goal is research output that could increase U.S. manufacturing competitiveness, there may be more focus on product traits which importing countries want, manufacturing efficiencies, and transportation. More faculty-monitoring of foreign journals, printed or via the web, will likely occur.

In the private sector, virtually all goals focus on output (including output efficiency and sales) and are measurable, such as lowering production cost on a soft drink line to X cents or increasing territory sales to Y dollars or Z units. Salary, promotions, and bonuses are based on such. Even in the federal government, staff are rewarded with bonuses. As an assistant secretary, I had a block of dollars to reward individual staff or teams for outstanding work toward agency missions and goals. A bonus rewards without locking in a higher salary base!

In this increasingly entrepreneurial management of universities, a bonus might well be considered when a faculty member brings in a large block of grant funds or establishes and publishes a major breakthrough in his or her discipline. If that is done, though, be sure there is some bonus money—and that it is used—for the teacher who publishes an outstanding work or devises and implements a new and effective teaching technique or advising system!

A few university faculty and administrators are bothered by goals, especially those that are measurable. I pressed one of my new deans to set some specific goals for his college. After a few weeks, it was evident he was uncomfortable with the measurable part, but he promised to continue with the task. A month later he reported that a series of discussions with his staff had resulted in four or five program "thrusts," high-priority areas on which research effort would largely focus. He had made some progress, but not enough.

Why would some want to avoid goals? I have heard two reasons: (1) Basic research is to simply "understand the nature of things," with the hope and expectation that there will come unanticipated but real and valuable advances to humankind. (2) Discoveries in metal properties, psychology, or nutrition (or other) may confront industry and social traditions that inhibit or slow implementation. Measurable progress toward an impact goal may be years hence. My answer to those objections: "Every discipline has benchmarks. A good scientist or unit head knows the discipline and the research sector—and also the benchmarks.

People in the discipline should write, or help write, the goals, including the measurement criteria!"

I believe there are some additional and unstated reasons: (3) Specific goals may imply boundaries that faculty or units do not want. (4) Measurable goals might not be met. Proud people do not want to risk failure. (5) Some may fear their specialty or personal priority will not be among the university's or unit's goals.

In regard to the latter, one of my better but smaller SDSU departments, Dairy Science, did not see itself in our top ten research goals. So, I added 10 more, including dairy efficiency. Though 70 percent of the base budget and all the new program money would go to the top ten, I made it similarly clear that I expected this smaller department to remain high quality, doing valuable work for its limited industry. Sufficient of the remaining 30 percent would be provided and faculty would be rewarded for excellent work.

Faculty, department heads and, especially, a president's administrative team of deans, vice presidents, and provost need to be involved in setting institutional goals and the major goals for major units. Your task, as president, is to see that the goals get set, that they are consistent with the institution's mission, that they are directional and, to the extent feasible, that they are measurable.

One should avoid the "blue sky" goal statements, such as "to become the best" or to "be the most highly respected university in the Northwest." That latter phrase might sell as a "vision," but it has little value as a goal. It provides no meaningful direction and there is certainly no credible way to measure. Such statements give no focus guidance to faculty and no guidance to department heads and deans in faculty recruitment, in charging them to high priority tasks, or in allocating appropriated and overhead funds. As important, because any progress made is so amorphous, little success can be demonstrated to the university's public, and little satisfaction can be felt by faculty or, especially, by a president or unit head!

CHAPTER 17

Demonstrate Accountability

Students of former President Harry Truman recall his scathing letter to a *New York Times* music critic after the critic's review of daughter Margaret's initial operatic recital. In theatrical depictions of Truman's life, the most poignant scene is Truman at his desk in the West Wing, when he seals the envelope containing that letter, then pulls and affixes a stamp from his billfold. It was a personal letter; Truman did not consider using the White House franking privilege. Nor did he give the sealed envelope to his secretary to find and affix a stamp.

A long-time director of a university veterinary clinic once told me about being chastised by his president for not having sent a bill after the president's dog was treated in the clinic. Soon after the next president arrived, his dog was brought to the clinic and the director followed up with a bill. He was chastised by that president for *sending* a bill.

Behavioral expectations start at the top; a leader's behavior is observed and long remembered. Your behavior, statements you make, positions you take, questions you ask, and what you reward each send important messages and can have much influence on faculty and unit accountability. That influence can spread through the system, helping insure that the total university is most accountable to students and other clientele, as well as to state and federal taxpayers.

In the early 2000s, the media were packed with stories of corporate misbehavior—Enron, Health South, Qwest, Alelphia, WorldCom, AIG, and even government-initiated financial corporations, Freddie Mac and Fannie Mae. Financial data were shaded and assets' sales were reported as operating income. These and other improper practices inflated reported profits and stock prices and, in turn, triggered heavy bonuses for top executives. Top corporate leaders misled investors and risked jobs and retirement benefits of employees. Even audit firms and lending banks were alleged to have helped implement or hide some of the immoral and illegal executive behavior.

I have seen no summary of the educational background of the several schemes' alleged initiators and perpetuators, but most are university graduates. Specific state universities have been mentioned in regard to a few. Although more column inches have been devoted to those trained in finance, accounting and law, no discipline for which universities educate is immune from the risk of graduates, or university staff, "pushing the envelope" too far in terms of what is ethical and credible.

A study financed by the National Institutes of Health (NIH), reported in the journal, *Nature*,[13] and covered by the *Wall Street Journal*[14] and other popular media, raises considerable concern. Of 3,000 researchers in the study, 6 percent self-reported they had failed to present data that contradicted their own previous research, 10 percent said they had inappropriately assigned authorship credit, and more than 15 percent indicated they had changed their study design or results in response to funding source pressure!

Consulting in the private sector can broaden faculty perspective, provide vivid illustrations for classes they teach, and enhance the university's reputation in that sector, but there are some credibility risks. Potential for conflict of interest—or the perception thereof—should be given careful consideration.

A recent nation-wide survey indicated that fifty-two percent of college and university students had cheated on exams.[15] Surveys on individual campuses and within disciplines have reported from thirty-four to more than sixty percent having admitted to cheating. What is the responsibility of faculty, as both teachers and models? Students get behavioral signals from their instructors and advisers. Young faculty watch senior faculty for behavioral signals. All faculty watch department heads. Department heads watch deans, and deans watch vice presidents, provosts, and presidents.

I once scanned the travel expense voucher of a key administrator, noted the trip was on a week-end and to a city where he had a child in some school competition. I asked one of my finance staff to take it personally back to the administrator with a two-part question, "What university program is this voucher related to and do you really want it to go forward?" There was reported a hesitant but red-faced response, "No, it was a mistake," and he tore it up over the waste basket. He learned a lesson.

Some may wonder why a president or dean would spend time reviewing expense vouchers. Although department heads, deans, or presidents may routinely delegate this to an associate, people at every level need to know that prudence is expected and monitored, at least on a random basis, *by the person to whom they report*.

After noting several financial problems in other universities, as well as my own, especially in auxiliary, foundation, and government grant accounts, I established early in my presidency an internal audit position. Half of the auditor's time was to be devoted to random work he or a central university officer would request; the other half was available to any dean or department head for accounts or activities for which they were responsible. An internal auditor need not be limited to money issues; audit capability should be available for random program audits, such as summaries of student success rate, research output, or statewide impact.

Do expenditures from auxiliary, foundation, and government grant accounts have the same approval requirements as for state-appropriated funds? Unfortunately, on some campuses they do not; to avoid risking university or staff embarrassment they should. Such funds exist for university-related purposes; supervising officers' responsibility for these funds is no less than for state-appropriated dollars.

Nor are universities immune from unscrupulous vendors. Some assume that university people are so focused on their own work they will not check quality—or numbers—of delivered materials. More than once my staff rejected No. 3 quality (lumber, for example) requisitioned to be No. 1. Demanding accountability is respected.

To what extent is the university accountable to enrolled students? Do deans and department heads know their student drop-out rates? Or graduation rates? Do they know the proportion of junior-senior or freshman-sophomore student credits taught by senior staff vs. instructors vs. graduate assistants?

During my faculty years at Iowa State, a considerable amount of my time was budgeted for academic advising of students from the freshman through senior years. In an adviser meeting near the close of fall term, Associate Dean Louis Thompson shared several (unidentified) freshman schedules, ranging from 12 to 18 credits, which advisers had approved for the spring term. He also showed each student's ACT scores and high school grade average, then asked, "Why would Student A, with ACT scores in the 30th percentile and a C average in high school be enrolled in 18 credits, mostly rigorous courses? Why would Student B, with ACT scores in the 90 plus percentile be enrolled in only 13?" He had our attention. There may be reasons, but they needed to be good reasons.

Do individual colleges and departments budget faculty time for advising? Does each have some measure or monitoring of adviser effectiveness? Is there a credible system of teacher evaluation? Asking some questions early in your tenure lets staff know accountability is expected.

Should a state university carry on research where findings are held confidential to the funder? It may be warranted and within board-approved policy, such as in the case of federally classified work or where external funding pays all costs, including substantial overhead for use of public facilities. However, where some of the cost is attributable to public funding, facilities, faculty time, and utilities, failure to report, delay in reporting, or selective reporting is improper unless it is based on fully considered and established university policy.

Do faculty get their research papers written? Or, do they procrastinate in writing, move on to the next project and leave the data on the shelf? There are exceptions, but my expectation is that for each piece of funded research, there should be publication—printed or electronic—in three versions, a paper in a refereed journal, a piece in a practitioners' or professional periodical, and a media release for the general or related public. In the case of grant and contract research, the funding agency usually monitors; the university—department, college, or research unit—should, as well.

Back to focus on you as president: How do you demonstrate personal accountability? One way is by being sure that your fringe benefits, whether from university or foundation sources, are spelled out in the employment agreement with the board. For your protection, copies of appropriate authorizations should be provided to the chief financial officer and any other people who may handle a portion of those benefits. For travel or other reimbursement, you should insist that all submissions be scrutinized before sign-off by a finance officer who is willing to bring back any item a critic might think questionable or inadequately documented.

Should you be elected to a corporate board, is the compensation to be kept or should it be given to the university or its foundation? The university governing board should establish the policy and I suggest it should be consistent with university policy for faculty consulting.

Because you, and perhaps other top officers, host official guests at sports and cultural events, you may be provided a block of tickets at no cost. That is totally proper, in my opinion, but it is well to find any written policy on such and to review it for prudence and propriety. When I arrived as president, my athletic department was so far in the red, it needed all the money it could get. I paid.

Except for football or basketball coaches or some medical school staff, the president is likely the highest paid member of the faculty. Other faculty may pay fees for use of the recreation center, university pool or golf course. If so, should not you?

And, in case you want to pen a personal note to a friend between scheduled office conferences, I suggest you carry some stamps in your purse or billfold.

So much for "early actions." The next section is more general, some experiences and suggestions regarding management functions.

PART IV

The Management Function

*W*ebster's *Collegiate Dictionary* defines the word, lead as: To guide; to direct in action, thought, opinion. For the word, manage, it has: To direct affairs, to achieve one's purpose. Some say leadership and management are a continuum, and I agree, but I separate the two functions in order to focus, in this and the next section, on what a president and management team *needs to do, or see gets done, to achieve the purpose* of the university.

The leadership function, clarifying the "great vision" that guides and sounding the call—challenging faculty and university supporters to pursue that great vision—has been underlined in some of the previous chapters. This group of chapters assumes the university mission and goals are established and that you, as president, have established the administrative structure and team. It focuses on the management that the university and its publics may expect.

One of my staff, focused on internal university management tasks while I had spent most of a week speaking to alumni and industry groups, used the steam engine illustration to remind me, "The steam that blows the whistle doesn't turn the wheels!" He was turning the wheels, making things happen, while I was out sounding the call.

You may spend relatively little of the 55-plus-hour week on what is defined above as management. Of all the program judgments to be made in a state university, resource allocations, personnel issues, and problems to be handled, most are delegated to others. However, it is an unwise president who delegates all management functions. And, that portion of time that you devote to management, essential to *achieve the purpose*, had better be quality time.

CHAPTER 18

Management Expectations

As president of Kansas State University, in my orientation welcome to incoming students, I listed some things each should expect from the university—quality instruction, an adviser who knows each student and the student's abilities, accessible library, complete recreation facilities, and exposure to diverse thought through faculty and guest speakers.

The university, conversely, expected some things from each student. I would list mature attention to studies, knowing and using one's adviser, using the recreation and library facilities and, especially, letting an instructor know when a lecture or lab experience has been especially good.

My daughter, with successful management experiences in the health care industry, once shared with me her practice of stating such expectations each time she moved to a new management position: "This is what you should expect of me and this is what I expect of you." I did the same in each successive management role in federal agencies. It was extremely helpful; it clarified, and avoided uncertainty.

Were I to assume a university presidency today, here are some things I would tell my central administrative officers and my deans they should expect of me:

1. To be guided by the university's stated mission.
2. To express my goals and to see that university-wide goals are developed, kept current, and pursued by the total university.
3. To delegate and to be specific in that delegation.
4. To seek and allocate resources in accord with mission and goals.
5. To give each one timely feedback, both positive and negative.
6. To be available for reaction, counsel, and support.
7. To give undivided attention when they bring problems or issues.
8. To be consistent and solid in decisions and commitments.

9. To be loyal to each and support their reasonable judgments and actions.
10. To share what I learn and observe outside the university.
11. To reward, with commendation, recognition, and appropriate salary.

This is what I would expect of them:

1. To be guided by the university and college missions.
2. To have clear unit and college goals, to see that they are kept current and pursued.
3. Loyalty to the university, to me as president, and to others of the administrative team. If someone disagree with my judgment on an issue, to tell me, not others. The same with their administrative colleagues.
4. To function within the delegation given.
5. To allocate resources within their unit in accord with mission and goals.
6. To face issues; to address needed refinement and change.
7. To keep me informed on issues, opportunities, and problems, and not let me be surprised by an outside source.
8. To develop and build management skills in their staff.
9. Willingness to travel. For deans and department heads, to spend time with their industry or profession, employers of their graduates, users of their research, and funders of their programs, including potential donors. For other units, such as finance, facilities, library, etc., to observe how comparable units function.
10. To encourage and reward quality work, creativity, and innovation.

Missions and goals are discussed elsewhere in this work, but with individual persons I would likely discuss each unit's mission and goals, to insure we are both "on the same page."

Delegation is basic to timely and effective university management, as well as for the satisfaction that each level of management deserves. The next two chapters speak to the effectiveness of and satisfaction derived by delegating.

CHAPTER

Delegation

For those continuing in an administrative post when you assume the presidency, habits and authorities are not easily changed. If, for example, your predecessor has delegated virtually all decisions in academic programs or budget, it may not be easy to pull back those prerogatives that you want and need. Your delegation to each person, therefore, needs to be specific and sufficiently discussed so that mutual understanding results. I suggest that you and each continuing person start from zero, with candid discussion and a new job description. When there is full understanding and agreement on that new description, all affected people should get a copy—and be helped to understand the new role and delegations.

People new to the administrative team should have no habits related to their post. Each will more easily play the role a new president wants.

A provost, vice-president, or dean wants responsibility and appropriate authority for decision-making, but does not want to over-step and have a decision reversed. Nor do you want your management responsibility and prerogative usurped. A good provost or vice president knows, from those candid discussions, when "it's the president's call."

The very title of provost, vice president, or dean conveys a delegation message, but for each, elaboration is needed. For example, a provost plays a key role with deans, but in choosing a new dean I worked with the provost in naming the screening committee. When the committee neared completing its task, the provost and I met with the committee to hear individual member comments about each of the top five or six candidates. The provost and I would then decide who and how many would be interviewed. After gathering staff reaction following interviews, the provost and I would make an offer, including salary, terms, and the task ahead.

For choosing new department heads, except in rare cases where I might need more involvement, I wanted reports from the dean and provost on progress. If an on-campus promotion was the dean's choice, I wanted the dean to bring the person to my office for a visit about the department and the task ahead before the dean made an offer. If off-campus people were considered, I wanted the same office visit with the top two or three.

For faculty appointments, except for cases involving leadership of new or major programs and distinguished professorships, I wanted to see a copy of the appointment form after sign-off by the provost.

To what extent are initiation and approval of new curriculums and programs—or termination of such—delegated? These represent long-term university direction and continued resource allocations. Such issues therefore need to be vetted and concurred in at the level—dean, provost, and/or president—appropriate to the magnitude of what is proposed. Only then should individual course or facility changes be advanced through any curriculum committee or research coordinating process.

How about major university councils and committees? Who names the membership? Who outlines their responsibilities and to whom do they report? Much of a university's program and policy development occurs in councils and committees. As a new president, you cannot afford to let yourself be cut out on items in which your leadership and involvement are needed.

Delegation of the authority to initiate, approve, or disapprove is a separate issue from "need to know." To avoid confusion and save everyone's time, *both* need to be spelled out in the delegation process.

As a president, you cannot avoid responsibility for everything that happens in the university. However, both you and your provost can make your lives easier and, no doubt, make "administration" more responsive, by letting deans and department heads manage how the mutually understood missions are to be pursued and unit goals achieved. That is the premise for the next chapter.

CHAPTER 20

Let Deans and Department Heads Manage

Early in my SDSU deanship, President Briggs declared that because of limited funds and public concern the university would hold the line on out-of-state travel for the next fiscal year. After studying the travel needs for each of my departments, I reallocated travel money. I increased some and decreased others, but left the college total unchanged. Budget documents were sent forward to the university budget office.

When my copies of the travel budgets came back with Director of Finance Wes Bugg's signature, all the increases had been lined out but the decreases approved. I took the budget sheets to President Briggs and protested; I had been asked to manage and Bugg's interpretation of his declaration had negated my management judgments. He quickly agreed.

There is a limit to the management judgments that can be wisely made at the top. That limit is often exceeded in universities (and, I assure you, in federal agencies). A president, provost, or even a university system office may issue an edict that all vacant positions are frozen, all travel is cancelled, or no equipment can be purchased when a severe budget problem arises. I have often wondered why. Especially in times of budget constraints, the most knowledgeable people, closest to the problems and most aware of the options, should be making—and taking responsibility for—the critical discretionary judgments *within the reduced or constrained unit budget.*

When there develops a presidential or systems office concern that university programs are not current, there might be a declaration that X percent of every college's budget shall be "re-allocated." I have often wondered why. If one or more colleges' programs are not being kept current, a president and provost should exert pressure on those colleges, where the problems are!

Several reasons are often given for such university-wide or system-wide pronouncements: (1) It is an emergency; rapid action is necessary. (There were likely some warnings that gave time to identify, by e-mail and telephone, any units or programs that should be protected from anticipated cuts or freezes.) (2) Fairness. (Is it fair to freeze vacant positions in College X that has increasing enrollment when College Y has no vacancies and falling enrollment?) (3) All position control and the salary budgets are really held in the provost's office. (Then why have deans and department heads?)

Deans and department heads have high motivation to provide effective instruction, productive research, and effective education or linkages to statewide clientele. They likely know best where the most productive work can be achieved per dollar spent, where efficiencies can be found, and where money can be saved with minimum cost to the mission. They have their students, their industries or professions, and their own units' pride to satisfy. Deans and department heads should have the flexibility, within university-wide policies and *within the resources allocated, obtained from external sources, or reduced,* to make the judgments that will best serve their constituencies.

If, based on enrollment trends, societal research needs, or proportions of tenured faculty, a department needs to limit new hires to nontenure track, close a program, leave a position vacant, or terminate nontenured faculty, such *is* likely worthy of dean and, perhaps, provost/presidential judgment. That may be the case in several departments. However, a university-wide pronouncement to freeze all vacant positions or cancel all travel invariably brings howls of unfairness. And, invariably, multiple exceptions to the pronouncement must be granted, and that results in more howls of unfairness.

Similarly, a pronouncement to revert X percent of every unit's budget to a central office for "reallocation" suggests there may not have been periodic dean or provost/presidential review of the program direction, work loads, or needs of *individual* departments or colleges. If a research project, extension program, or a curriculum needs to be closed out, or a new research project, extension program, or curriculum needs to be established, that should be faced directly. Money, positions, grant-seeking effort, and/or custodianship of facilities should be shifted by the department head, dean, or president/provost to effect the change. Such should be met and handled by the appropriate administrator(s) and, in some cases, with consideration by appropriate councils or committees. It is rarely well served by university-wide, umbrella action.

A recent example: As this section is being written, I learned of a major university where a new president and new provost declared that henceforth "no interim dean nor department head will be considered for full appointment to the position." A caution as to the risks of interims being eligible for full appointment may be in order, but to forever preclude consideration unnecessarily cuts off options that may, in some cases, be beneficial. A university may be best served to leave options open for judgment input from deans, department heads, and faculty in individual cases.

I offer two additional reasons for letting deans and department heads make more of the discretionary judgments; both should be very important to you and your provost. (1) When deans and department heads make the judgments, they carry the responsibility. They take some of the heat off of you and the provost. (2) Deans and department heads get more mastery of their units' destiny. If they make a good decision, they can feel pride. Why should key administrators be denied that opportunity? Such is fitting reward for the daily burdens they carry.

Chapter 9, Study the Data, lists considerable data that a new president should review. Such data for colleges and departments are equally valuable, or more valuable, to deans and department heads. They are the ones who will likely effect any change that such data suggest is needed. I therefore urge that they receive the data pertaining to their unit—and perhaps data that show how their units compare to others—at the same time (or before) it goes to you and/or the provost.

Suppose the data show, for a college or department, a considerable number of courses dropped on account of low enrollment, extraordinary faculty turnover, student drop-out rate twice the university average; or that all freshman and sophomore courses are taught by instructors and GTAs, while associate and full professors average but a six-credit teaching load. Suppose the data show only two refereed journal papers by a department in the past three years. If you want a dean or department head to address such an issue with enthusiasm—and gain some satisfaction from doing so—that dean or department head needs to have time to analyze the data, consider the reasons, and make some judgment about what can be done to improve the situation *before being accosted* by the provost or president with the data.

Letting it be known that you and the provost are reviewing a specific issue, and studying related data from the office of institutional research, guarantees that each dean and department head will be checking out the data to see how their unit "stacks up." A week or so later, for units where some problem appears to exist, a meeting can be scheduled with the dean, or by a dean with a department head, to "get their input and thoughts." Invariably, the dean or department head will come with their analysis of the data, the reasons for it, and some specific steps that have *already been considered or implemented* to address the problem.

The dean or department head can then be commended for taking the initiative. If such has not occurred, another problem has been identified.

Additional management strategies are discussed in the next chapter.

CHAPTER

Management Strategies

"Be poised to pounce!" A financial consultant with whom I have worked in management seminars often repeats that statement. "Have enough free cash and borrowing capacity to pounce when you see supplies, property, or a business you can buy for cents on the dollar." The principle applies in a university. A president should have enough accumulated goodwill in the governing board, governor, legislators, and perhaps foundation board; enough talent in the management team; and enough flexibility in the budget and operating policies that when a golden opportunity appears, the university can take advantage.

Michigan State University (MSU) leaders had long wanted a law school. But, with an outstanding law school at sister University of Michigan, such appeared out of the question. Along came evidence to MSU President Peter McPherson that the private Detroit College of Law, 90 miles down the road, was in accreditation difficulty because of inadequate library and other issues. MSU had excellent library resources. Discussions were initiated.

The result? The College moved from Detroit to the MSU campus and MSU underwrote a bond issue to finance a new building for the College. The name, Detroit College of Law, was retained, but MSU named a third of the College's board. Today, it is the Michigan State University Law School and almost completely integrated in the university. It yet has a separate board but, by formal agreement, follows the policies and procedures of the university. This further closeness came at the request of the law school.

At Kansas State we needed to increase our "presence" in the metropolitan Kansas City area to attract more students and political support. State universities in rural settings, common with land-grant schools, can be handicapped by their distance from the states' urban centers and the continuing rural to urban population shifts. Such was certainly the case with Kansas State, 70 miles west of Topeka, on the Great Plains side of the Kansas Flint Hills. Wichita, the state's largest city, had Wichita State University, and the University of Kansas was between Topeka, approaching 100,000 in population, and nearly a million in the greater Kansas City area.

Kansas State's only specific programs in the greater Kansas City area were county extension offices/programs and a much-appreciated graduate education program—evening and Saturday classes—provided by our college of education. Our strategy added several initiatives: (1) A charge to a new dean of Architecture to develop semester and summer courses and internships in Kansas City, Missouri (No Missouri university offered architecture and Kansas in-state tuition was granted to Missouri residents.). (2) Strengthen extension programs in horticulture and horses. (3) Develop articulation agreements with metropolitan community and two-year colleges. (4) Establish a part-time recruiter stationed in the Kansas City area. (5) Build stronger relationships with key legislators from the area.

Tradition and geography made it a steep hill to climb, and we encountered some roadblocks. Kansas State is part of a six-university system with a single governing board, and board members were concerned about curriculum duplication, especially off-campus. They noted our willing and ambitious Education faculty driving by the University of Kansas to service the greater Kansas City area and thwarted that program. The architecture program thrived and, although we could not quantify the relative affect of each effort, enrollment from the Kansas City area steadily increased. And, we credit Kansas City area legislators for some large legislative victories, including a line item budget for Veterinary Medicine and a couple of major buildings.

Management and efficiency, words so common in the private sector, are generally not popular words among academics. To some academics, they denote control, standardization, and quantification. "A university is not a factory!" you hear when there are efforts to quantify workload, seek more efficient ways to teach students, or measure research output or impact. "We focus on quality, and you cannot put that in columns to tabulate." However, you, as president, and others of your management team cannot abdicate such responsibility.

One of my most rewarding experiences and of most benefit to faculty and students during my dean years resulted from comparing numbers of each department's FTE instructional faculty with the number of courses, as measured by course credits shown in the university catalog. It was a measure of faculty time required to keep course content current. We found that listed course credits *per FTE instructional faculty* ranged from 21 in one department down to seven in another. No wonder some faculty were complaining they had too little time for their research or to advise students! As serious, some courses had not recently been taught; they had been promised by the catalog listing, but routinely cancelled for low enrollment. Students had been misled!

After discussing each department's data with its faculty, Associate Dean Burt Brage and I gave each department with a high ratio of course credits to faculty a *reduced limit* to the number of course credits it could list in the next catalog. Faculty retained total prerogative to select and organize the material into the courses that would be taught—*as promised*. A department with increasing enrollment and, consequently, added staff, was encouraged to add courses in priority topics.

The point of this illustration is certainly not that the president or provost should devote significant time to addressing such an issue in departments. You should be looking at university-wide and college data, the latter to determine that deans are attentive to efficient use of faculty time and keeping faith with students.

How does one assess teaching and curriculum effectiveness? Feedback from employers and graduates certainly helps. So do exit interviews with seniors and those finishing graduate degrees. I also endorse well-structured systems of student evaluation of teaching and advising, as well as administrative review of course outlines, teaching portfolios, and faculty writings. A visiting professor reminded us in a seminar on effective teaching, "Department heads and deans imply an assessment when they recommend salary increases. Does it not make sense to have input data and judgment from the students?"

Assessing research output and impact is another challenge. Whereas many universities highlight "research activity" in publications, presidents, provosts and deans need measures of research output and impact. I am exceedingly proud that in FY '05, the department in which I now hold a collaborative professorship, Animal Science at Iowa State, had 140 peer-reviewed publications, an average of 2.64 per faculty member.

How about citations, which imply impact on the scientific community? Within certain disciplines, data on the number of times certain of a universities' publications are cited is available on a web site, www.in-cites.com. As with other data collection and survey, there is some limit to this site's comprehensiveness or coverage.

Copyrights, patents, and genetic releases by the university show potential impact on an industry or society. If data can be gathered on distribution of copyrighted material, sales of product by the companies to whom the patents have been licensed, or acres in the state planted to a released wheat variety, the university— and its funders and supporters—can have some measure of its *actual* impact.

Peer pressure can be effective in helping achieve research output and impact. During my direct leadership of research as a director, we printed in our bi-weekly staff newsletter a brief report—dollars and FTE spent, plus publications and other measures of output and impact—each time a project was closed or ready for renewal. Exposure of that information to fellow faculty and staff did more to encourage publication than any cajoling by department heads or my office.

Money for travel, new equipment, and teaching or laboratory supplies are critical to faculty productivity. To help productivity, my guide is that not more than 70 percent of a university's operating budget should be devoted to faculty and staff salaries. Within programs, I suggest 70 percent in instructional operating budgets, 60 percent in research budgets, and 80 percent in Extension education budgets. Obviously, the optimum percentages will vary among universities and disciplines. However, I have yet to find a university with less than 80 percent of its budget devoted to salaries, and well above 90 percent is common.

Budgeting state and overhead money, or seeing to it that grant proposals provide funds for technicians and other support staff can allow more effective use of a strong research professor. Travel, supplies, and equipment are essential for effective extension programs. The same is true for instruction: support staff and facilities can assure more effective illustrations in the classroom or laboratory and higher quality professor–student interaction.

How do you, as president, and how do your deans and department heads achieve a needed shift in extension education, research, or curriculum? This is no different than guiding staff in any other business or profession: (1) focus on mission and goals; (2) charge, reassign, and retrain (use sabbaticals aggressively) existing staff; (3) hire and charge new staff when opportunity permits; (4) allocate or remove money and/or facilities; and (5) commend, recognize, and reward.

Chapter 8 described how Iowa State's Vice Provost for Extension Stanley Johnson shifted his state and overhead funds toward the units and programs that had successfully increased grant and fee funds for certain programs. By doing so, he speeded the shift toward activities which society had prioritized in the federal or state appropriation and private investment processes. His reasoning: Should not the staff and those programs be further rewarded? That strategy has its limits, of course, but some programs that were dropped or reduced by half evoked essentially no complaint from clientele.

What about high quality tenured faculty in a curriculum or program no longer needed or afforded? As a dean, I moved a poultry geneticist to teaching introductory biology; poultry genetic line development had moved to the private sector. He found a brighter future, his expertise a "demanding market." He had more students to teach and more satisfaction at the end of the day. There was a bonus for the students—vivid illustrations; every biology student can relate to birds and eggs.

Such relocation to a different department and building can sever attention from decade-long routines, accumulated data, and old problems. For a good scientist, there can be a renewed challenge and greater reward. And, a significant university benefit results.

In all management strategies, goodwill, finesse, and sensitivity are needed and pay dividends. Pride is important. A chance to succeed is important. Loyalty to students and clientele is important.

University management need not and should not be abdicated. Resources are too precious and product quality too critical. Society needs more highly educated people and there is more knowledge to expose; Mother Nature's Book of Knowledge has many chapters not yet read.

With deliberate strategies, universities can be managed by presidents and their management teams, some of that management exercised in the process of just "walking around." That happens to be the title of the next chapter.

CHAPTER 22

Walk-Around Management

Wwhile walking the USDA halls one morning for short visits with staff about their work or issues of the day, I heard Dr. Val Mezainis, my head of global research, refer to it as "walk-around management." It is an apt term, and I had learned its value my second week as a college instructor. I had noted my department head standing in my open classroom door. In a moment he moved on. My reaction? Positive; he was interested in teaching—and in me!

Information you, as president (or provost or dean), need often gets filtered through an administrative structure. Some people will tell you more in their office or the hallway than they would in your office. And, many staff will never *get* to your office.

A dean or department head can show you the college or department facilities, cramped or spacious; you will see the staff's working comfort or discomfort, and note staff interactions or a "go-it-alone" tendency. If at the right place at the right time, you might see a near-completed student project or in a research lab microscope how living cells interact. At Kansas State, I would often plan my route through the bakery management hallway—an instructor might need a second opinion on student product!

Especially important, you will better understand the issues and problems that department heads and deans daily face, and perhaps find out how they or their ingenious staff have solved some of those problems. Invariably, you will find opportunities to commend innovative teaching, research, or management, and perhaps be able to commend one of the maintenance staff on building cleanliness or appearance of the grounds.

Perhaps as important, those deans, department heads, and staff will have feelings paralleling those I had that day I saw my department head standing in my classroom door. They will know, "The president is interested!"

You should not overlook the placement office, the health center, or the carpentry shop. Joining the buffet line in the student commons will be noted by both the students and commons staff. Eating with a few students has another plus; you will learn what is really going on in the classrooms and otherwise on campus.

"Walk-around" may include a seminar, a staff retirement or recognition event, or a student club meeting. This does not necessarily mean speaking at the event. Kansas State's revered Dean Weber once cautioned me, "Your presence is often all that is needed." You cannot attend every event or, in a large university, spend significant time in every unit. But word of a president's visit gets around—rapidly. By the end of the week, after Provost Koeppe and I had visited a couple county extension offices, staff in most of our 105 county offices likely knew about the visits. They also knew that we recognized the important role of county staff in the total university.

For issues on which later action may be needed, an unsafe laboratory building, staff distressed over poorly ventilated classrooms, or other, having been there to see and hear may enhance your confidence in making a decision or approving a recommendation. Further, periodic appearance throughout the university helps fill the need that each faculty and staff member has to feel an integral part of the total university. And an hour out of office, with or without a dean at your side, is a refreshing break.

CHAPTER 23

Innovation

Change that responds to new economic reality, social priority, demography, or technology is rarely initiated in the middle of a successful industry. Most core businesses continue doing what made their industry or business successful. Where there is responsive change, it invariably happens *first* on the *fringe* of that industry, discipline fringe (tax law vs. accounting in business structures), the cultural fringe (Microsoft vs. IBM), or the geographic fringe (North Carolina vs. Corn Belt in swine production). People on the fringe think "outside the box;" they are not "in the box."

Higher education has parallels. Within some colleges and departments, we see a failure to respond to new economic reality, social priority, or other. In others, there may be rapid response. Some colleges of medicine and veterinary medicine adapted early to the greater depth of available technology in the broader biological sciences by hiring other than MDs and DVMs on their faculties. Some resisted well into the latter half of the twentieth century, insisting that every faculty member had to have an MD or DVM degree. The former, generally, made the greater advances in training their students and in their research. The latter lagged.

Colleges of education, public schools, and education organizations are under a critical public eye at this writing, especially in the teaching of reading, but also in other areas. Yet, our U.S. education system had all the earmarks of success in the country's early years. Have we not tapped professionals, concepts, or ideas from diverse disciplines and settings, such as human motivation, social marketing, social sciences, human nutrition, physiology, or psychology to the serious business of education?

A department or college with a global reputation and with tenured faculty who helped make that reputation may have difficulty "turning the ship," reallocating time and resources. What society sees as an emerging need, the university or one of its units may not see. Or, a department head, dean, or president may see it, but appear unable to "turn the ship."

On this topic my mind returns, with considerable embarrassment, to a stairway conversation, that I had when dean, with one of our extension faculty at a state cattle feeders' convention. We had just listened to a discussion of feedlot run-off problems and the possibility of state regulations. I suggested we should collect run-off data from existing feedlots, especially the amounts of nitrogen and phosphorus, and use the data in educational meetings and publications. If producers had the data, they could more wisely plan new construction or renovations to avoid stream pollution problems. His response? "If we collected the data, it would just prompt those regulations. Nobody in this business wants regulations."

Today, virtually all states plus the federal Environmental Protection Agency (EPA) have regulations on feedlot design, location, and capacity. Further, many of those regulations are without a scientific database! And, in the meantime, some of my friends have paid heavy fines for nutrient run-off and resultant fish kills in the streams.

Why did I not press that issue more aggressively? What kept us from shifting resources and reassigning university engineers, chemists, and animal scientists to collecting the data? Did we not see the societal concern? Did we not recognize that the trend toward concentrated animal operations would intensify the problem?

What kept individual faculty from re-directing their own efforts? Wanting three more years' data on a current project? Comfort with current activities? Or was it "loyalty" to an industry that did not want regulations?

How about fertilizer and pesticide run-off from cropping operations? Were our entomologists and agronomists tracing the fate of products not absorbed? Or, were we fearful we would find data our strong agricultural clientele would not like and that we would risk their political support? Faculty at Indiana's private Wabash College were gathering such data!

Is there today, or will there be tomorrow, a parallel issue facing your dean of engineering, business, medicine, or social sciences and their faculties?

The *earliest* responses to changed demographics, industry shift, new societal problem, or political realities often occur on the "fringe" of a department or college— a university discipline that seems hardly related, an independent research institute, an economic development agency, or a private business! For example, which university department first included in their undergraduate courses the physical consequences of workers' repetitive motions in office work or manufacturing? Was it industrial engineering—perhaps the university department closest to affected industries—or was it business management, sociology, or physical therapy? And, did that response come first within the university, or was it forced or prompted by regulations or external pressures? Similarly, was research money and faculty time reallocated for needed research or did that await the appearance of a targeted federal grant program?

If the response comes early within the department central or close to the affected industry, it may well be triggered by new faculty members with a background and experience considerably different from that of senior colleagues. They may have a different socio-economic background or come from a distant region, where the related industry is less dominant. They may have their degrees from a different type university or in a discipline different from the core of the department that hired them. And, although the response may come, the road is not easy. If such a new faculty member challenges colleagues' postures, will he or she risk tenure?

A state university has a tremendous breadth of disciplines and talented staff in each. What a great place to tap knowledge and concepts that are needed to address an emerging societal or industry need! Any department can find in other units, if not its own, faculty "on the fringe" of its central disciplines. Biomedical Engineering grew out of joint effort between colleges of engineering and medicine, veterinary medicine, or biology. Who first saw the need, an engineer, a physiologist, a surgeon, or a private sector client? Which scientist first walked across the campus or to the next building to solicit help? To a biologist or a mechanical engineer, the other's discipline may seem distant, but the need that physically handicapped people, prosthetists (those who work with handicapped people) or equipment and machine designers have for knowledge of human movements and human – machine interactions dictates a close working relationship between and among these and other disciplines.

Bioinformatics got its start from a variety of disciplines, discipline needs, and technologies, including genetics. Mapping a species' genome involves millions of data points. To manipulate that data volume for the purpose of understanding genomics of a species—the degree to which individual DNA segments influence phenotypic traits—requires computational, statistical, and biological concepts and skills. To each of these disciplines, at best, the others are on the fringe.

For innovation in the instruction and curriculum arena, federal, state, or industry grants are less common than in research. However, most provosts maintain a "new ideas" or comparable fund to finance new and experimental ventures. Some deans and large departments do the same; more should. I have observed that most colleges and departments have more budget and staff flexibility than they use; tradition often controls budget and time allocations, and opportunity for innovation is missed. Perhaps two sections of a limited-enrollment course can be combined and staff time freed to prepare a new course component. Perhaps a creative instructor just needs a word of encouragement to teach that new course she proposes *beyond* her normal teaching load.

Constraints are not just about money. Requiring college or university committee approval can also inhibit teaching innovations. I urge a policy that allows a one- or two-term offering of experimental courses under some generic catalog number for which the approval of only the department head (or dean) is needed.

Those deans and departments—and their faculties—that allocate funds and FTE for such or for new instructional techniques and demonstrations, who initiate effective student advising systems, who eliminate redundant administrative procedures, or who find new and more effective ways in any university endeavor should be commended. Those who reach across unit lines to capture the skills and diverse disciplines they need and recruit new faculty with discipline talents and interests needed for emerging issues should be commended.

I believe that the greater ethnic and racial diversity existing today among both faculty and some management teams, and the increased numbers of women in fields traditionally occupied by men, and of men in fields traditionally occupied by women, are valuable contributors to innovation. We each "see the world" differently. The more diversity, the more views of an issue, the more awareness of diverse or emerging needs, and the more conviction and support there may be to address those needs.

A university management team should also reach beyond the university to government installations and to foreign institutions. In the food and agricultural disciplines, a dozen or more "international agricultural research centers," scattered among Peru, India, Nigeria, and other countries and financed by multiple governments as well as the World Bank are valuable sources of both concepts and genetic materials for U.S. university programs and clientele. In the physical and biological sciences, an increasing volume of the cutting edge work is in the private sector. Joint ventures, industry–university work groups, sabbaticals, and travel opportunity in and with the private sector can keep faculty exposed to the latest in that discipline.

Iowa Regent Gartner suggests, in regard to universities as elsewhere, "Change has no constituency." To the extent a "change constituency" void exists, *department heads deans, provosts, and presidents should fill it!* Perhaps, as a new president, that is one of your coaching duties, the topic of Chapter 24.

CHAPTER 24

Coaching

While a young associate professor, riding across the Argentine pampas in the back of a little French Citroen with my dean, Iowa State's Dr. Floyd Andre (we were on a curriculum review assignment), I listened as he recalled and described in rather vivid detail a series of thorny personnel issues he had handled, one just down the hall from my office. I wondered, "Why is he telling me all this?" The day we returned from Argentina, my mailbox contained a letter inviting me to interview for the associate dean position at Kansas State. He knew that invitation was coming; he was coaching me. In the years ahead, I was to encounter every type of personnel issue he had shared—and more.

Coaching is every administrator's responsibility. As president, coaching your team members demonstrates your interest in their success. The same holds true for a dean or other officer, coaching his or her team members. With your team members' success, the university and each unit or sector of responsibility may be stronger. And, with those team members' success, you, as a "coach," can feel some extra satisfaction.

A few months after arriving as dean of agriculture and biological sciences at SDSU, I had a call from Governor Nils Boe, "Our pheasant population is down and that will hurt businesses all across the state this fall. Some conservation people are blaming the fertilizers and chemicals our farmers are using. Is that the problem? I want you to get to the bottom of it."

I needed some coaching and asked Biochemistry Department Head Oscar Olsen, who had served as interim dean, for advice. He suggested I call the state director of Game, Fish, and Parks and propose that we bring our scientists together to present and discuss their data. We did, and the data clearly showed the pheasant decline to be part of a normal population cycle. Together, the director and I gave the governor his answer. Coaching is not always from the top down. We may learn from our experienced colleagues or from outside the university.

The first example in this chapter illustrates the coaching opportunity that travel provides. Away from the campus and scheduled meetings, there is time to let thoughts and reminiscences flow. Distant examples are instructive but non-threatening. Perhaps as important, one-on-one travel conversations invariably fill the gaps in acquaintance—where and how each was raised, significant events that molded motivations, perhaps even aspirations for the years ahead. To effectively coach, one needs to know well the person being coached.

How do you get to know well a key member of an administrative team? Obtaining the information described in Chapter 6 is a start, but there often remain some voids. One of my unit heads and I were having trouble seeing eye-to-eye on several issues. I had an evening talk scheduled in Wichita to a group in his field of interest, so I invited him to ride along. The two hours each way "opened a lot of doors" for communication. We got better acquainted. It helped.

As president, you may take the provost, vice presidents, and deans on a several-day state tour and seminar. I suggest you pick a section of the state, a comfortable retreat for the overnights and the seminar part, and ask each of several deans to arrange an hour or two-hour stop en route, perhaps at a clientele business or profession, exposure to which would benefit the group. Such might be a venture capital firm, a bearing plant, a community college, a banker, or a government agency—whatever.

A legislator or a university trustee on the route might be invited to host the group for coffee and a visit. Anyone in the state would be honored to host such a group. And they will be most generous in telling *their* university's management team about their business or profession, how important the university is, and what they expect of it. They may even share some management anecdotes.

My first effort at this was as a dean. When I suggested the idea, a couple of more senior department heads were less than enthusiastic, "I don't know if we can afford four days away from the campus." I did not press, just took my three associates and the four department heads that had been in their jobs less than two years; they would benefit most. We visited a forestry demonstration project, a cheese plant, a high school, a large farm supply and grain marketing cooperative, and a bank, and spent time with the managers of each. We had a day-long seminar on instruction, research, and extension, a free-flowing discussion. We talked about the roles of the associate deans vs. those of the department heads. We talked about some problems and opportunities that faced the college and how we should approach them.

On our return a couple senior department heads inquired of one of my associates, "Why weren't we invited?" The next time, a committee of two senior department heads, along with an associate dean, planned the four-day tour. This time, the agenda included a visit to a commercial game preserve on the Pine Ridge Indian Reservation, time with our extension staff on that reservation, and a Native American lunch, complete with "fry bread" at a local café deep in the Dakota Badlands.

Far more than coaching, growth in management skills, or exposure to a state's diverse features can result from such travel time as a group. With meals together, a few hours in a car, and an evening on a lake shore fishing or just visiting—and learning that an administrative colleague has similar challenges—can do a lot to build esprit de corps.

Are there certain topics or skills on which an individual colleague needs some coaching? One of our dean candidates, an outstanding scientist and teacher who had performed exceedingly well in earlier administrative posts, was nearly rejected by our screening committee because of his reference, in the interview, to "the outstanding work of a couple of girls among my current faculty." He needed some coaching on terminology—and he did an extraordinary job as dean. This experience reminded me of the importance of coaching. Lack of earlier coaching risked his advancement to a dean position and our missing his valuable leadership.

It may be well to review the data in Tables 9.2 and 9.3 in Chapter 9 and to study comparable data for your university. Do the trends—increasing proportions of certain racial or ethnic groups and women rising through the professional ranks—suggest focused attention on identifying and coaching certain persons as potential members of your administrative team? On a national basis, according to Chapter 9 data, it seems to me that it does! What do the data for your campus suggest?

How about administrative internships? Some find these very constructive. I have seen people move from these, directly or indirectly, to successful administration and they express appreciation for the experience. However, I offer some words of caution. Academic people are high-pride people. To accept such a precisely titled "administrative internship" carries some risk. What if administration proves not for them? Is the host administrator willing to share all? If the internship limits the work to one supervisor, it can be a narrow experience. And, an intern can be an "errand runner."

An early administrative experience needs to be carefully structured and a less precise term than "administrative intern" might be considered. There are other options for experience and coaching, such as membership on or chairmanship of curriculum or other major committees or councils, or special leadership assignments.

Some people seem to be born with good personnel and management skills. Most of us are not. But we learn, if we have had challenging experiences and good coaches. Universities need all the management skill that can be found and developed. All members of your management team carry responsibility to not only coach current colleagues, but to help identify and coach some of the next generation. As part of that coaching, I suggest that you purchase several copies of Flawn, Budig, Shaw, Crowley, Collins, or Sample (all listed in Bibliography or Additional Readings)—or this book—and give one to a each of those faculty or junior administrators you think could benefit higher education even more by their moving into or upward in administrative roles. Doing such is a part of coaching; it prompts such promising people to consider their potential and to give thought to enhancing management skills.

The next chapter is titled, Feedback. Are not coaching and feedback the same? They are certainly related, but I believe they are not the same and each is important. I define coaching as building and strengthening a set of skills that can be used in any number of circumstances. Feedback I define as a response to a specific circumstance, perhaps an event or an action. Feedback is an integral part of program leadership, supervision, and staff evaluation.

CHAPTER 25

Feedback

Early in my presidency I became distressed that long-time Finance Vice President Dan Beatty—highly respected and completely loyal—had not made a change I had told him was needed to solve a serious problem. When he saw my distress he was surprised, "But you didn't pound the desk and say **get it done!**" I learned my feedback had to be more emphatic.

One of the most competent and professional directors of university information with whom I worked in universities seemed to worry continually about whether his work was adequate. Regular feedback, a word of commendation or satisfaction, was important.

To a greater extent than the average of society, university people are proud; they expect to be successful. Although they may respond more quickly to feedback, the form of that feedback merits thought. Some are highly sensitive to criticism, and that pride and sensitivity may be the reason some university administrators avoid candid feedback, even in an annual performance review. They may fear embarrassment, anger, or, at least, discomfort.

Where feedback is absent or limited, there is left a large void in "How am I doing?" Opportunities to enhance both performance and staff satisfaction are missed. Where feedback is steady—a word of encouragement, a question or expressed reservation, a public or private compliment, or your interest in a problem that needs attention, and commendation when it is well addressed—the annual performance review can become almost a formality. There will be no surprises, nor fearful anticipation. Rather, the performance review will merely reinforce the year's interaction. A dean, vice-president, or provost should look forward to their annual review with you. So should you.

Each of us may recall the events or comments that inspired us to do more, to do better, or to alter our teaching, research, extension, or administrative work. Odds are high that most were received in situations *other* than in an annual performance review.

As president, you will receive plenty of feedback regarding the university, staff, programs, and your own decisions and actions. It will come from faculty and students, parents, athletic fans, and the local community. Some will be in the form of editorials. You will feel good when the feedback is complimentary; you will be an exception if all of it is.

You need to be cautious in dealing with complaints from persistent "squeaky wheels." Check things out before drawing conclusions. Do the same for complaints about "the high flunk rate in Department X" or about the utterances of a dean or a faculty member.

I had flown to the Custer Game Lodge in the Black Hills to speak to the North Central Extension conference, and the first person I encountered in the lobby was a friend from graduate school days. "How's it going, Mike?" I asked.

His response was a glum "Not very good," and he handed me a letter: "Read this." It was his copy of a letter from his dean to an industry leader and it said, in part, "Rest assured that this college and this university does not endorse the comments made by Professor X at the _____ meeting in your community last week. We are in full support of _____ ."

Mike followed up, "The dean didn't even ask me if I had said what I was accused of saying!"

"Check it out" before responding.

Feedback helps keep each person on track and can provide a lot of encouragement to each along that track to be more productive and to gain more satisfaction. Feedback needs to be early, understandable, honest, and thoughtfully offered. Of course, you must follow the basic rule, "Criticize in private; commend in public."

Feedback you receive may well identify and quantify some university problems, a few of which are illustrated in the next chapter.

CHAPTER 26

Addressing Problems

Here are two contrasting cases, both real.

A Sociology department head marched into his dean's office about 10:30 the first day of the semester, "One of my students just told me her genetics instructor said that anyone majoring in sociology, physical education, or journalism just as well drop the course; they won't be able to handle it." The dean called the genetics department head with two requests: (1) Ask the instructor if he said what was reported, and (2) if so, solve the problem—"or I will."

On another campus, an English instructor repeatedly came to class inebriated. Students complained to the department head and dean's office, but there was no action. Eventually parents sent complaints; still no action. The dean not only refused to address the problem or see that the department head did, but he protested that parents "have no business telling the university how to handle its faculty."

By addressing such a faculty problem, you can either increase the instructor's value to the university or encourage the instructor to seek another occupation or setting that is "more fitting to their talents." Avoiding the problem is not fair to the students, the university, or the instructor! I do not know the fate of the English instructor, but in a visit to that genetics instructor's campus four years later, I inquired. He was a highly respected and appreciated teacher.

How about problems in university business procedures, campus maintenance, or office and classroom comfort? The University of Minnesota did a classic study of departing faculty from their Minneapolis/St. Paul and Duluth campuses. It was several decades ago and I do not find the reference, but the two major reasons given by departing faculty apply today in both universities and businesses: (1) "No one told me I was appreciated until I resigned" and (2) accumulated frustrations, such as classrooms that are too hot or too cold, delayed expense checks, or snow-clogged parking lots.

Every large organization seems to have plenty of the latter, seemingly minor problems in the total university context, but they frustrate faculty and staff and those frustrations accumulate. And, how often do we neglect to take the time for the former—telling a colleague or faculty member how valuable he or she is?

When a dean or a government agency head has lamented to me about seemingly never-ending problems coming to them, I have often responded, "That is why you are there. Problems exist to be solved and I think you are the right person to solve them." And, to solve some of them, a manager may have to track the problem *through the system* to its real source.

Though we had made our college budget allocations within days of April adjournment of the Kansas legislature, budget work sheets were not getting to deans and department heads until weeks later. With the fiscal year starting July 1, they were too pressed for time, and were frustrated.

Budget Director Ted Dodge—most conscientious and always wanting to accommodate—reported, and Vice President Beatty relayed, that his budget staff just could not get the work sheets out faster. I pressed; there had to be a root source to the problem.

There was. A long-time budget office clerk was still using a hand-based system she had been trained to use before electronic equipment arrived: she felt comfortable with that system. Beatty and Dodge just had to confront the problem.

Soon after my February arrival as vice chancellor at Nebraska, Research Director Howard Ottoson briefed me on a problem in Plant Pathology over the naming of a plant disease, a specific wilting of the corn plant. Professor Max Schuster had identified the causative organism and, with that accomplished, the disease could be formally named. A faculty committee considered several names and chose, instead of one recommended by Schuster, Goss's Wilt and Blight (Goss was a former graduate dean and plant pathologist who had apparently studied the disease in earlier years). Department Head Mike Boosalis had approved the committee recommendation but Schuster was distressed, and there had been heated exchanges.

Over the next several months, from Ottoson's and Boosalis' comments, it appeared the problem was not going away. The stress continued, and was affecting the work of both Schuster and his colleagues.

In the meantime, Horticulture Department Head Joe Young, who was working hard to build a department research program, had commented to me how much he appreciated the work Schuster was doing on some ornamental diseases. (The two departments shared a building.)

When I got the next report of friction in Plant Pathology, mid-summer, I gathered Ottoson and College Dean Ted Hartung, "Let's go solve the problem. Bring Schuster's project budget sheets." We alerted Boosalis and Young and gathered in Schuster's lab. In 30 minutes, we had identified which of the department technicians worked most closely with Schuster, discussed his current work and budget, and made the decision to transfer him, one technician, and the lab from the Department of Plant Pathology to the Department of Horticulture. Ottoson would work out research budget details with the two department heads.

The Plant Pathology department no longer had the daily friction, Schuster had a new relationship, and Horticulture had a larger research portfolio. The pay-off for me, though, came a month or so later, at the fall semester faculty reception. When the Schusters came through the line, Mrs. Schuster squeezed my hand and mouthed a quiet, but intense "Thank You!"

A construction superintendent at a business in which I am involved shared with me his philosophy, "If you don't solve the problem today, it will bite you tomorrow." However, a problem on a six-month construction site is different from an administrative personnel problem in a university unit, especially one with statewide clientele.

While dean at SDSU, I had commented to President Briggs about foot-dragging by an across-campus unit head with whom some of our faculty had to work. And, there appeared to be an alcohol problem. It was obvious that I wondered why he was still in the job. President Brigg's response included some wisdom, "Every unit head has their constituency. Sometimes you just have to wait until that constituency sees the need for change."

Months after that conversation, I came to realize the degree to which one of my own department heads was stifling needed change, and I asked leading questions of both faculty and industry leaders across the state. One industry person summed up what I was both observing and hearing, "Prof is a wonderful guy, but he is the type that will ride a train facing the rear so he can see where he's been." I had my answer; the time had arrived.

Perhaps the most difficult personnel problem I encountered as president involved the leadership of our agricultural programs—my own sector of experience and four people I had long known and respected! Vice President for Agriculture Roger Mitchell, the top officer, had been hired and arrived a few months before I was named. Continuing in their positions were College Dean Carroll Hess (instruction), Experiment Station Director Floyd Smith (who'd been acting vice president for an extended interim a few years earlier), and Extension Director Bob Bohannan. Each position had long carried full budget authority, from central allocations for instruction and with line item appropriations for the latter two.

Most faculty positions were joint teaching-research or research-extension, so department heads had to negotiate among the three—Hess, Smith, and/or Bohannon—on new appointments, salary, and promotions, and sometimes for operating funds. In essence, department heads reported to three people. The Vice President had a title, but no budget, and so little operating authority, even to settle disagreements among the three. Frustration was apparent in all parties, especially the department heads.

In time, Bohannan returned to a faculty position and was replaced by John Dunbar, from Purdue. Stresses continued and, in time, became more severe.

All officers were experienced, conscientious, and with sincere motives. But, with strong personalities, considerable seniority in second-level positions, and each party having some constituency, several attempts at solution had failed. Frustrations, both on campus and off, demanded a solution.

I named a small ad hoc committee of top faculty, industry leaders, and students and asked for their advice. It did not take long for them to consider the issues and options, and to give me succinct advice, "There has to be one boss in the agriculture programs; do what you need to do to achieve that."

Effective the following January 1, we eliminated the four positions and created, effective that date, four new positions, a dean and three associate deans, with the dean, by job description, to have full budget authority (and to delegate as appropriate). We then formed a search-and-screening committee for the dean position and, subsequently, for each of the associate dean positions. Each of the four existing officers held a tenured professorship in an academic department and, if not selected for one of the new positions, would move to that professorship.

Although all involved went through a rough time, each of the officers "landed on his feet." Mitchell was invited back to the University of Missouri, from which he had come, as Agronomy department head and, within months, was named dean and had an excellent career in that role. Hess took an assignment in the United Arab Emirates, an assignment so productive that it was extended, and Smith renewed his well-deserved reputation in soil fertility research, just at a time when increases in crop genetic yield potential called for reassessment of fertility levels. Dunbar was named to fill the dean's role until his retirement a few years later.

Department heads henceforth had one boss. For faculty and clientele: "Case closed." All could focus on program.

Could such a circumstance and career-affecting consequence have been avoided? Yes, I believe it could, and I offer the following illustration for how: Suppose you need to hire a new dean (or other top officer) and one or more associate deans are in place. Do not "just hire a new dean," but address the *issue* of the total administrative team. *Before* a new dean is recruited or selected, I suggest you and the provost make it clear to the "associates" that they should expect a new dean to have considerable privilege in determining the subsequent administrative structure and pattern of delegation. The situation parallels that for a new president with a provost and vice presidents in place (See Chapter 14). A new top officer has to have some prerogative in team structure and operations; once that prerogative is exercised, "administration" can be more productive and rewarding to all parties.

The issue for you, as president—and for any other member of your management team—is to face each issue, to make *both* the solution judgment and, in most cases, the timing judgment. Where a significant constituency is involved, timing may be dependent on how well that constituency *sees* the problem vs. how long the system can *tolerate* the problem. To not face the problem is an abdication of responsibility.

Another of the problems that presidents and their management teams may face, with budget pressure, enrollment shifts, and changes in research or extension needs, is that of combining or closing units or programs. Such warrants the next chapter.

CHAPTER

Combining and Closing Programs

Closing or combining programs (units, departments, colleges) is seen by some in university leadership the way Social Security is seen by most members of Congress—as the "third rail," not to be touched. However, if programs are low on society's priorities or significant benefits can be achieved by combining units, *it is no secret!* If you (or provost or dean) see the reality, so do others!

Closings and combinations can occur but, as with people problems, each program or unit has its constituency and loyalties. Process and timing are important.

I have been involved in closing two university research facilities, five pairs of university departments (on three campuses), and two pairs of divisions within a federal agency. Later, I handled the first steps in combining two agencies, serving as administrator of both during the process. (The formal combination could come only after key members of Congress could consider and accept the consolidation and, by then, I had moved on to the assistant secretary role.)

Major keys to getting needed closings or consolidations done are:

1. Full information on the opportunity and/or need;
2. Early conversations with key legislators, clientele, and, in certain cases, community leaders.

Two more steps are, in many cases, equally important:

3. A new and challenging assignment for affected staff; and
4. Commitments—dollars or other—to new programs that may have more value to students or clientele than the units or programs closed.

Two of our SDSU off-campus research stations were of limited value: the areas' needs had changed. Budgeted funds could be used better elsewhere. One, which focused on grain and swine production, was especially important to its host community for both employment and pride. My first step, after concurrence in the plan by President Briggs, was personal visits with the local state senator and state representative. After I shared my assessment and asked their advice, each told me who else I needed to talk to and each assured me they would not protest the closing.

The next step was a meeting with invited agricultural leaders in the area the station served. We had earlier assured the superintendent continued employment at another location (Step 3) and he as well as our Extension leadership and related department heads were involved in that leaders' meeting. We posed the station closing issue and asked, at the same time, "What are your highest priority needs from the University?" The response was quick and consistent among attendees, "Demonstrations and extension programs on grassland and cow herd management." After an hour of discussion on details of what they said was needed and ways of providing that, we committed, on the spot, dollars and staff time, and even identified the faculty member who would likely lead the efforts (Step 4). That seemed to clinch acceptance of the station closing, and the cost of the new effort would be but a fraction of the station's annual budget.

At the end of the meeting, one of the younger and more outspoken of the group caught me at the door, "What took you guys so long; we haven't used much of that station's work for several years!" Long time Ohio State Dean Roy Kottman once observed, "The backlash tigers we fear often turn out to be paper tigers."

More than once, in consulting with universities, both in the U.S. and in Eastern Europe, I have encountered research facilities that, for prudent management of dollars and faculty talent relative to industry needs, should be closed or the total program changed. However, fear of political backlash from the community, current industry leaders, or legislators made presidents, deans, or directors reticent.

Faculty can create backlash, and probably will, if they have not been consulted, if their pride is tied up in the unit and, especially, if they have had no assurance of their future value to the university. I have also seen several instances where leadership completes Step 1 and initiates Step 2. But, in carrying out Step 2, they miss some key people in exploratory or briefing conversations or meetings. Or they are not ready to take Steps 3 and 4, make commitments to affected staff or to a higher priority (and perhaps less costly) program that clientele need. A premature announcement or a meeting "to discuss" ends with the clientele or faculty feeling suspicious; turmoil follows, and the plan to close is abandoned.

In general, to avoid trauma in combining units, the same steps are needed as with closings. The situations are parallel in terms of pride and service to students or clientele. After plans were announced to consolidate Animal Science and Poultry Science at SDSU (both with departing heads returning to faculty positions), staff of the smaller poultry department came to my office with the concern, "Will we get buried in this combined department?" My response, "Productive faculty members don't get buried." However, to assure both them and their industry clientele that I recognized their importance and the value of their work, I made a commitment: For the next three years, the proportion of appropriated and overhead funds to poultry work would not change. After those three years, "all bets are off;" the new department head would have full prerogative in developing and recommending the departmental budget allocations.

In department or college consolidations, faculty worries often center on losing identity and, consequently, on the name of the combined unit. Iowa State recently combined the College of Education and the College of Family and Consumer Sciences. When consolidation was proposed, there was understandable concern by a good many alumni, especially those of the latter college, in existence as Home Economics from the university's early days. However, with committee work over a two-year period in developing guidelines for the consolidation process and in choosing the resultant name, Human Sciences, the consolidation appeared to occur with little visible pain.

A budget crisis can make closings and combinations easier. Both clientele and staff will more easily accept such changes without a feeling of leadership failure on their part. My first assignment in USDA was to head an agency that was over-organized and overstaffed relative to its fiscal year budget. Six divisions reported to me through two assistant administrators. About a month into the job, I invited all staff, including secretaries and part-time people, to meetings where all budget and obligation data were put on the blackboard and solution options were openly discussed.

Following that meeting, we implemented the only realistic solution. We terminated temporary staff, out-placed 15 civil service staff to other agencies, and consolidated the six divisions into four divisions reporting directly to me. We then had enough money to finish the fiscal year and also buy some needed PCs. There was a bonus; with one less administrative layer, we had a more responsive organization both internally and to clientele.

If the focus is kept on better serving students and clientele, insuring challenges and satisfactions for faculty, and if solid commitments are made to insure that good and perhaps new things can happen, needed unit closings and consolidations can be made. Faculty and clientele admire positive management leadership. Faculty will endorse and support change, if fully informed, involved, and, especially, if their subject matter prerogatives and their levels of satisfaction can be preserved or enhanced. So will clientele, if you can prioritize what they say they need and their leadership pride is not damaged.

PART V

Sectors and Issues

While serving in Washington, my wife and I were invited to a one-man, hand bell concert, and the concert artist was our former Manhattan "neighbor boy" turned church music director, Kevin Shull. Concert hand bell music normally spans three octaves with 13 bells in each octave! But Kevin handled that long table of bells so deftly we could be captivated by the music, almost oblivious his physical movements.

As I later considered that performance and Kevin's shift of total focus to each bell, I thought of my university presidency days, moving my focus from one issue or sector to the next, perhaps several in an hour, many in a day. Just as Kevin had to be comfortable with the weight and tone of each bell and their contribution to the melody so, too, do you, as president, need to have some comfort with each of many sectors and their contributions to your university's total functioning.

Some days you will feel you are moving among issues as rapidly as Kevin was moving that day among the bells. However, you are not a one-man or one-woman performer; you are more like the director of an eight-member bell choir. Each member of your management team carries the major role for certain issues or sectors; you lead and orchestrate. But to do that well, you need to know each sector and have reasonable comfort in dealing with issues in that sector. The chapters that follow will, I hope, contribute to your—or other top officers'—comfort in dealing with some of the major university sectors and issues.

CHAPTER

Complementarity of Instruction, Research and Extension

ssociate Professor Julia Badenhope in Iowa State's College of Design recently told me about her satisfaction in working with city councils and private landscape architects on enhancing the appearance of Iowa town entrances. She had a significant grant from the state department of transportation—probably funded by Congress' highway appropriations—for the work. I asked if she had some of her undergraduate students involved. "Oh, certainly," she said, "their involvement is part of my satisfaction."

The most enthusiastic instructor I had encountered in my undergraduate days was Dr. Damon Catron, who taught the junior-level course in animal nutrition. He not only showed enthusiasm for the discipline, but also for the animal feed industry, comprising companies that formulate and sell nutrition supplements and rations for livestock, poultry, and companion animals. He was doing research and he told us about it. He was consulting with the feed industry and he told us about it.

A few years later, as an instructor in Oklahoma State University's meat processing labs, my students and I processed animals from the department's research projects, including one project that I was leading. We discussed the variations in leanness and calculated the value of retail product as influenced by the experimental diets.

During my teaching years at Iowa State, I handled a number of extension night meetings, workshops, and summer livestock tours when our department had extension staff vacancies. Producers would ask me some tough questions. I would see a variety of production systems and bring vivid illustrations back to the classroom, as well as some researchable problems for my colleagues. The complementarity of campus instruction, research, and statewide extension activities was evident almost daily.

I was surprised, therefore, to later find in some universities the animal science extension faculty both organizationally and physically separate from the instruction and research faculty. One university had made the separation very clear, with a separate Department of Extension Animal Science.

About that time, however, the U.S. government had asked the University of Illinois, Kansas State, and several other U.S. universities to help India, Nigeria, and other less-developed countries relocate and consolidate their ministry-managed research institutes and extension programs with major teaching colleges. Those countries wanted to replicate the teaching-research-extension benefits of U.S. land-grant universities. It was also about then that we were on the Argentine Pampas designing an animal science master's degree curriculum at Pergamino, a major research and extension station. Industry leadership had concluded the "teaching" university in Buenos Aires could not get the job done; faculty there were neither up-to-date on research nor in tune with industry practices.

With federal contract and grant programs for research and technology transfer or extension-type education in virtually every discipline—from nanotechnology to childhood education to environmental issues—and considerable support from state agencies and the private sector, few disciplines in any state university need be without the mutual benefits that result from having and meshing these multiple functions *within* a college and department. To the extent feasible, I believe most individual faculty should have instruction, research, and extension responsibility. If faculty are separate in duties, they should at least office in close proximity to one another. Research focus is more likely kept in tune with industry, profession, and society needs. Both students and state-wide clientele will benefit from their instructors being on the "cutting edge" of knowledge. There is another bonus to the department from statewide extension-type faculty activity—student recruitment!

In disciplines where lack of funds preclude formally organized extension-type activity or research, other means of interaction with related professions or industries should be encouraged. The English faculty may write for publication and edit for publishers or for writers like me. The music faculty may perform, write, lead workshops, or handle music therapy programs. The foreign language faculty may translate for industry conferences or consult with travel agencies and immigration support services. Professional consulting should be encouraged.

More federal and private research funds flowing into colleges of engineering or arts and sciences, or to departments of biology, mathematics, physics, economics, or other means more intellectual vitality in the total department. However, a problem can result; the attention and support a dean or department head can give to the teaching program may be limited. For research activities, facilities need to be modified, laboratory equipment purchased, grants renewed, matching funds identified, and links with off-campus clientele maintained. Support to instruction, advising, student recruitment, placement, and related activities can get shortchanged.

Agronomy, my largest department at UNL, was in that circumstance; Department Head Don Hanway, an outstanding leader, just had too much to do. I urged him to pick a top person in each of teaching, research, and extension for half-time program leadership in those respective areas. He was reticent, worried about spending too much of his budget on "administration." I told him to do it; I would take the responsibility. When those associates were named and in action, his staff got more rapid response and support, and Hanway became an even better department head.

Having worked on five campuses with heavy research and extension functions in many colleges and departments, having held most of the titles and having addressed some problems with the system as president, I suggest a basic format to maximize leadership and minimize frustration: The top officer at each level, department head or dean (in a few universities the top officer in engineering, medicine or agriculture may carry such a title as vice president), should retain responsibility for general program direction and budget allocation for all functions: teaching, research, and extension, delegating those responsibilities and prerogatives each feels is appropriate.

Department heads should report to and be evaluated by the dean. Deans should report to and be evaluated by the provost/president. The associates—associate heads, associate deans (or program directors), vice provosts—should be program coordinators and leaders, with whatever specificity in program and budget delegation their top officer may determine. In large and complex universities, that delegation will be large. The important issues are that teaching, research, and extension are coordinated—there should be just one decision-maker whenever there is a conflict or competition among the three sectors—and that deans and department heads each have that one person who carries the lead in their annual evaluation, that each have "one boss."

Now, let us focus on the student curriculum in the twenty-first century.

CHAPTER

Global Curriculums

After the close of a research conference in Mexico City, a French scientist and I were visiting the nearby pyramids. In a light exchange he asked, "What do you call a person who handles two languages?" "Bilingual." I answered.

"Three languages?"

"Trilingual."

"How about one language?"

I hesitated. "An American!" he exclaimed.

During my university and later government work in more than 40 countries on five continents, I do not recall being greeted by my hosts in any language but mine, English. As host to foreign academics and business leaders on a state university campus, however, the best I could do was to memorize a greeting in their language before their arrival. I am not proud of that.

The United States' massive economy and its physical separation from multilingual societies of East Asia and Europe have let us be self-content. We have been unduly so, given the global competitiveness and global opportunities that face graduates and the universities in the twenty-first century. If there is a "soapbox message" regarding the future of state universities advanced by the author in this work, it is that every university must equip its students for their professions, their businesses, and their lives in a global society and economy.

When I became administrator of USDA's Foreign Agricultural Service, I was surprised to learn that some young Foreign Service officers, most with master's degrees from strong U.S. universities, were being dispatched to foreign posts as assistant attachés without first mastering the language of their host country. The paucity of candidates with the needed language when a post opened had caused the agency to relax an earlier language requirement. Newly assigned attachés were being allowed to "study the language after arrival." For my time with that agency, the policy of language competence *before* being dispatched was reinstated. Intense training was needed and given.

For graduates in this twenty-first century, exposure is not just to another language. It is exposure to another, or more than another, society and culture—and religions are a significant part of most cultures. At one of the numerous dinners held by student groups on our campus, I was introduced, unexpectedly, to give a blessing prior to the meal. Having noted several Muslims and a Jewish friend in the gathering, I began with "May we each give thanks, perhaps to our own god, for —— ." At the close of the event, I received more appreciative comments for "including us" or "not excluding me" in that blessing than I might have received for a talk on which I had worked days.

One needs to know something of the culture to fully respect the culture. For the student, it is not just exposure to the culture. It is also some comparative global study in the student's discipline, their future business sector, or their future profession. For example, every major accounting firm in the United States has offices and ownership partners in other countries. Medium-size U.S. accounting firms outsource much of their work to firms in other countries where costs are lower. In 2003, an estimated 25,000 U.S. tax returns were done in India and 400,000 were expected to be done there in 2005.[12]

Virtually all U.S. manufacturers of significant size—and a high proportion of small manufacturers—export significant volumes of product. Many U.S. companies have production and distribution facilities in other countries. And, many of those that are recognized as U.S. companies are, in fact, subsidiaries of foreign corporations. U.S. engineering firms complete for and handle projects in many foreign countries. Some subcontract design work to firms in countries where salary and other costs for professional engineering are a fraction of U.S. costs. Foreign engineering firms compete for work in the U.S.

State university graduates—engineers, food scientists, business administration grads, and other—now supervise workers or manage plants in those countries. A number work there, or here, under European, Asian, or Central American supervisors. Electronic Data Systems and other U.S. computer service companies employ hundreds at facilities in India and elsewhere. Billions of dollars move electronically among countries on a daily basis. European banks have purchased some U.S. financial institutions. They and Asian banks are currently on the lookout for other acquisitions.

More than 50 percent of the items in some main street or big box retail outlets come from other countries. It is virtually impossible to buy a week's groceries or a season's wardrobe without a few items from Central America and/or Asia. Though the U.S. is considered a major exporter of agricultural products, a high proportion of the orange juice we consume comes in tankers from Brazil—and some soybeans for crushing travel the same route. The Pacific Northwest has long supplied other countries with high quality apples, but China now grows four times as many, and competes strongly with the U.S. in the global apple market. ISO (International Standards Organization, headquartered in Geneva) and other third-party verification systems that certify the production and handling procedures which global customers seek are commonplace in manufacturing, transportation, and even in the financial industry. Many global customers demand such.

Considerable attention has been given in most state universities to international experiences—internships, travel courses, semester abroad, etc.—for undergraduate students. Most have been initiated in the languages and the social sciences, but I have encountered U.S. education majors doing their practice teaching in London, England, and Christ Church, New Zealand. I am also aware that some professional colleges, from business to engineering to agriculture, organize and seek funds for international travel courses, and work with industries on internship programs for undergraduate majors. Other options exist: Engineers Without Borders-USA recruits and mentors about 350 engineering students a year to help develop infrastructure in about 40 countries.[16]

Iowa State's College of Agriculture reports that 20 percent of their senior class has had such an experience; the College goal is to double that. David Acker's (no relation to the author) recent promotion from assistant dean for international programs to associate dean for both instruction and international programs was a timely move that reflects reality and the College's forward vision.

How about individual courses in the curriculum? The Wall Street Journal[17] recently reported that to get licenses and permits to establish a new business in Brazil requires an average of 152 days vs. 58 in Mexico, 42 in China and 5 in the United States. The greater time requirement—largely bureaucratic impediments—is suggested as the reason Brazil's economic growth has lagged relative to its natural resources and other potential. Do political science, public administration, and economics courses outlines include such comparative issues? Do human nutrition courses compare food groups, diets, and eating habits and traditions—and their health consequences—in Central America vs. those of the U.S., Canada, and Eastern Europe? Does the pharmacy curriculum mention drug-approval criteria and procedures in multiple countries? Many U.S. citizens are buying their drugs from Canadian suppliers or sources in other countries.

For decades, Bath, England, has been a city planning model for students of architecture and urban planning. Are the more recent dramatic architectural achievements in Southeast Asia, Denmark, New Zealand, and other countries featured or analyzed in design courses? How about the recently completed water bridge (canal) over the River Elbe near Magdeburg, Germany? It is an extraordinary illustration for either an engineering or architecture course—or a transportation course in the business college.

How about the University's central learning resource, the library? Maybe the word, library, is the wrong name. As I spend time in university libraries, I note more students at computer terminals than reading books. Google recently began scanning millions of books held in five major libraries, to be indexed and available over the internet.[18] Although, at this writing, publishers have objected to the project as copyright infringement, technology and consumer thirst for access will somehow make such material available in "real time." Perhaps the library should be renamed "The Global Gateway."

The university itself is not insulated from that global competition, for both students and nonstate funding. During my time with the U.S. Agency for International Development, a major sponsor of students from developing countries, my colleagues and I openly discussed the relative cost to our limited budgets of financing those students at U.S. universities vs. some outstanding universities in India and elsewhere. If the purpose were simply education, we would have chosen some of those lower-cost options. However, an overriding issue was exposure to and student time in the United States.

How about privately financed students from China, South Korea, or Africa? U.S. universities compete with foreign universities for those students—and for some U.S. students! To address that global competition reality, several U.S. universities, including Duke, Chicago, Stanford, Northwestern, Cornell, Johns Hopkins, and MIT, have either established graduate campuses for certain curriculums or entered into joint ventures with universities in Singapore or Hong Kong.[19] Should not a state university consider such relationships?

What is your role as president (or of a provost, dean, or department head) in this global reality? The first is to think globally. It is to think of the global competition that your students, and the businesses and professions your students will enter, will face after graduation. You should see to it that your colleges and departments focus on preparing your students, undergraduate and graduate, for life in a global society and economy. That global society has multiple cultures and conflicts; that global economy presents both competition and extraordinary opportunities.

Were I, as president, to interview a potential provost, dean, associate dean for instruction, department head, or other top curriculum leadership officer today, I might ask to see his or her passport. I would like to see one that has been well used.

CHAPTER

Student Enrollment

ocal business and apartment owners will be happy when university enrollment goes up. They will be disturbed when it goes down, and they will let you, the president, know it. Regardless of a university's research reputation or economic impact on the state, some trustees, state budget officers, appropriations committees, and media will judge a university and perhaps its financial needs largely on enrollment.

Enrollment at any given time is a function of *both* student retention (success and satisfaction with the experience) *and* the number of new students who enter.

Retention. The early paragraphs of Chapter 9 describe the academic dismissal of Kansas State students who, according to ACT scores and high school transcripts, *could* have done well at the university with more effective advising. An adviser system and training program, including budgeted time for student advising, was implemented. In some cases, faculty FTE for advising was made available by more closely managing the number of course sections offered, reducing the number to actual need. Two years later, academic dismissals at the end of spring semester had dropped from the 95 to 77 (net student gain of 18). More important, voluntary dropout between fall and spring semesters, mostly freshmen, had dropped from 56 to 21 (net student gain of 35). An aggressive recruitment effort and two new curriculums had been implemented and fall enrollment increased by 156, but at least 53 (18 + 35) of that increase could reasonably be attributed to *increased retention*.

New students need an adviser who knows their academic capacities, who can call them by name, in whom they may confide, and whose advice they will follow. Advisers need to be chosen for personal skills and student interest, trained for the task, given procedural and information support, and be assigned enough advisees to become good at the task. To not budget faculty time for advising or manage the advising system is to not recognize its importance. If a student has chosen a college or a major, the academic adviser should be a faculty member in that college or major. Especially in a large university, the closer a student can be to their chosen interest—an adviser in that discipline and enrollment in at least one course in, or close to, that discipline—the higher the odds for success and persistence.

I certainly recognize that many students are undecided and many will change majors, some more than once. Until they choose a major, most effective advising may be provided in a "general college," or in the office of the dean in the college of their choice. When they choose or change their major, an adviser's files can easily move with the student to an adviser in the new major.

Some students drop out voluntarily, although doing well. Why? One of my staff interviewed 100 students near the end of their freshman year, asking a series of open-ended questions about what had made them content or frustrated with their college experience. The most consistent response associated with satisfaction and their plan to continue was their "being called by name" by at least one faculty member. Such recognition and acquaintance by a faculty member helped the student feel part of the university; they were not just a number or "one of the throng." The positive effect of being called by name by their adviser and/or at least one instructor, regardless of the course, was significant.

Recruiting freshmen. While outlining this chapter, I received an e-mail from Associate Dean Acker that said in part, "I convened a team this week to develop a plan for undergraduate recruitment for 2005–2006. We are developing a very aggressive program that targets Iowa, Chicago, and the Twin Cities (Minneapolis and St. Paul), several carefully chosen national targets (Puerto Rico, where we have a pretty good pipeline established, and California, where we have nearly 900 alumni), and several fairly sure bets internationally (Korea, Thailand, Japan, and China). We want a bigger pool to select from and a more diverse pool to enroll. As you can imagine, much of our international diversity is at the graduate level. But at the undergraduate level, we don't have enough opportunities for Iowa's future agriculture leaders to rub shoulders with their peers from around the world."

Though chapter 13 mentions a chief marketing officer *responsible* for student recruitment, aggressive recruitment and follow-up by the subject matter college or department, in most cases, is vital. Most prospective students heading to engineering, architecture, law, pharmacy, agriculture, or certain other professional schools will tell you they are going to college to *become* an engineer, architect, etc. In contrast, more students who choose liberal arts go to college "to get an education." However, I believe specific interest—in history, political science, physics, speech, or other—also exists among many who are headed to the liberal arts. Discipline contact in the recruitment process will more likely "make the sale," and the effectiveness is enhanced even more if the faculty member making the contact is likely to be the prospective student's adviser.

You need to make clear that student recruitment is a responsibility of every college and every department, and not limited to central "student recruiters" and the admissions office. For effective student recruitment, university-wide or by a college or department, the following rank high among influences:

1. A good job of teaching, in all disciplines.
2. A good job of academic advising, and other student support.
3. Spirit and enthusiasm among current students. That comes largely from the first two. That spirit, where it exists, is generously shared with younger siblings and friends.
4. Contact and follow-up by the admissions office, deans' office and department staff.
5. Financial aid, especially where there is competition for top students.
6. University involvement in high school college days: science fairs and music, debate, and sports tournaments.
7. Contact with and information to high school teachers of individual disciplines, as well as guidance counselors.
8. University open houses; sports, debate or music camps; 4-H conventions; and science fairs.
9. Close relationships with community colleges, including development of integrated curriculums.

A natural focus in high school relationships is the guidance counselor, but teachers in every discipline can have impact on college choice. I suggest you see to it that some university faculty in every discipline make contact with high school teachers related to their discipline—music, art, biology, mathematics, physics, chemistry, agriculture, economics, or other—and perhaps visit some high school classes. Every university discipline has a message or demonstration that can be of value to some high school class. High school teachers, as well as guidance counselors, have district and state meetings and may need a good presenter from the university.

Land-grant universities, with state-wide extension staff and offices in most or all counties, have a recruitment advantage. Extension staff contacts, their visible enthusiasm for the total university, and 4-H and other youth-related extension programs can effectively prompt or support a student's interest in and application to the university. Virtually every state university, however, has off-campus education and technology transfer programs. Faculty involved in these endeavors should be an integral part of the student recruitment effort.

Many state universities carry on an intense recruitment program—high dollar scholarships, honors programs, and repeated personal contact—to attract higher ability students. Such students will more likely succeed in the university, land good jobs and, in later years, add to the university's reputation. In the high schools from which they come, regard for their chosen university is enhanced.

Universities should expect and prepare for the mix and characteristics of their students to change over time—in race, ethnicity, curriculum interests, and perhaps other factors. Since 1970, women's undergraduate enrollment has increased more than twice as much as men[20] and Table 9.1, in Chapter 9, projects that by 2013 women will comprise 57.4 percent of enrollees.

Although current university attention, in those states with industries increasingly dependent on migrant workers (food processing and agricultural production in many states and housing construction in the southern states, for example), may be on continuing education for the workers and their families, the university should be building plans to recruit those families' children! In 2005, there were an estimated 14 million unauthorized immigrants (in addition to the many authorized immigrants) in the United States, more than half from Mexico, and a quarter from other Central American countries. The immigrant children are or will be in the U.S. primary and secondary education system; for many, university education will be their route for upward mobility.

In our dynamic, global economy, you should expect continued shifts in curriculum popularity and related job opportunities. For example, nuclear engineering was popular in the 1960s, but enrollment dropped precipitously through the 1980s. With recent increased costs of other energy sources and renewed interest in nuclear power, student interest is returning.

Financial assistance—scholarships, grants, work-study, tuition waivers, etc.—play a large role in recruitment. Net cost is the focus of most students and parents, but the recognition afforded by a scholarship is also a plus. Housing and food options may be important factors for some; the current student population expects more privacy, more options, more amenities, and more freedom (perhaps total freedom) from university regulations.

Transfer students. During my first tour at Kansas State as associate dean, my assistant dean, Frank Carpenter, worked with each Kansas community college to establish one-year or two-year curriculums that, when satisfactorily completed, would be accepted in their entirety as credit toward graduation in our college of agriculture. For each community college, considerable negotiation was needed on course content and course credits. Department X's curriculum may have required two four-credit chemistry courses and one four-credit physics course as prerequisites to upper class courses in the major. Community College Y may have offered a three-semester chemistry sequence totaling nine credits and a three-credit physics course. Would that suffice in Kansas State's Department X? College and department faculty needed to be involved in the judgment.

A community college catalog can state, "All credits in this listed curriculum will be accepted toward a degree in the College of _____ at _____ State University if the student completes all courses with at least a _____ grade average and transfers to the _____ State University within three years of community college enrollment." The university catalog can list the community colleges with which such transfer programs have been established. Tedious negotiations to achieve such take time and goodwill, but the result is a win/win! Such integration can help the community college attract pre-professional students and it can provide a flow of sophomore or junior students into the university's professional or other majors. Most important, no student—or their parent or community college adviser—need be surprised by a university's rejection of transfer credit for application in their chosen curriculum!

How about dual admission and enrollment, where the student is admitted to both institutions as a freshman? How about the university department granting collaborative faculty status to a top instructor and adviser in the community college's parallel discipline? Each may be another step to facilitate student flow to the university.

One more point regarding universities vs. community colleges: Several undergraduate advisers in universities have told me, and and performance data support it, that at age 18 young women are, on the average, more ready for the university. They are more focused and more ready to pursue higher education and a profession than the average young man. One phrased it this way, "Most 18-year-old girls are "young women"; in many cases, a young man of 18 is still a boy!" The adviser added, "The latter is more likely to enroll in the community college and, in some cases, aim for a terminal program." Such observations merit consideration; they may well influence recruitment and articulation efforts.

Graduate students. As an animal science teacher and adviser, I would often encourage a student interested in a master's degree to check out the animal science department at a smaller state university that did not offer the Ph.D. I knew each student would get full attention and support: they would not be competing with a stable of Ph.D. candidates. With a solid master's degree experience they could go on, if they wished, to a university and department that focused on the doctorate. A couple of smaller departments that I respected highly recruited master's degree students on that basis.

Students choose a graduate degree university primarily on (1) reputation of the department faculty and (2) financial assistance. Graduate student recruitment, therefore, is largely a departmental responsibility; the graduate school and admissions office may provide support. For departments with a strong national or international reputation, recruitment may not be needed. However, I observe graduate professors are always on the lookout for the top students both on their own and from other campuses. For those graduate programs relatively new or in disciplines where graduate school opportunities abound, aggressive department or college recruitment may be needed.

Other actors and factors. Current students are among the most effective recruiters. Who has more enthusiasm than freshmen or sophomores—or newly arrived graduate students—who are doing well? If they are given the tools and leadership, they will be effective one-on-one. You should also not overlook the potential help of alumni, university fraternities and sororities, and sports and other interest clubs. They seek new members and should be made a part of the effort. Also of value are campus events that recognize outstanding high school or community college students and that recognize high school and community college teachers and guidance counselors. For certain curriculums, the employing industry can be interested and helpful. They need well-prepared graduates in their future ranks.

New student enrollment is certainly influenced by pricing policy. Fees may be reduced for selected disciplines (or scholarship/grant/student employment funds differentially used) in order to attract enough students in a specific curriculum to achieve economies. In-state tuition may be available to students from nearby areas of adjacent states, or in curriculums not offered in nearby states. If such is the case, that fact needs to be well known. As in any sales effort, your university should find out what the customer wants and show them how your university can provide it.

CHAPTER 31

Research and Extension: Global and Local

At the China Academy of Science in Beijing and Huazhong University in Wuhan, China, in the late 1990s, I visited research laboratories at the cutting edge in tracing the genome of the human, rice, swine, and poultry. Interacting with research institutes and universities in 17 countries by e-mail, fax, and faculty exchanges, Huazhong faculty were beyond, in some instances, what I had been aware of in the U.S.

Virtually all of the commercial grain sorghum hybrids grown in the U.S. have their genetic roots in East Africa and southern Asia. Should germ plasm, now almost universally used in the U.S., encounter an exotic disease or pest for which plants in our "monoculture" are susceptible, we would be searching the USDA genetic banks for germ plasm from East Africa and southern Asia, or we would be in those countries searching their diverse cropping systems for resistant lines.

Whether it is rice genetics, manufacturing techniques (the most modern and efficient steel mills I have seen were in Taiwan), cloning (biologists' work with the potato at Kesetsart University in Bangkok in the early 1990s were even with or ahead of what I had seen in the U.S.), or other, U.S. industries and professional sectors are in vigorous global competition. To maintain or expand their customer base, they need to be equal to or one step ahead in new products, product quality, product identity, and trace-back capability, as well as in customer accommodation. This applies not only to manufacture of hard goods, but also to engineering consulting, food production and processing, containerization and packaging, software, electronics, banking, architectural services, construction materials, and diagnostic services—virtually every economic sector.

One might spend an evening with a dozen people brainstorming and identify no sector where the U.S. enjoys insulation from global competition. The sobering part for state university leadership is that the U.S. business and professional sectors depend heavily on new technology and concepts from state universities to help keep them competitive. If your university is to play well its societal role, it needs to be in tune with and ahead of its global competitors.

There is little merit in listing all the disciplines, private sector businesses, or government services where global acquaintance and information exchange is vital to research and extension faculty; a number were mentioned in the curriculum section. However, we can add a few for study and analysis: The trade policies of New Zealand and Chile compared to those of the U.S., water conservation techniques and the economics of such in Israel, fish and crustacea production of Southeast Asia, and the natural resource conservation policies of Swaziland. Your faculty may identify others.

The businesses and industries—and the policy makers in legislatures and agencies—to which your colleges and departments relate can provide and should be asked for advice and counsel on research and extension education agendas. With rare exception, each industry's or profession's global competition will be reflected in the advice offered. Faculty exchanges, sabbaticals, e-mail, and electronic and printed journals provide limitless opportunity for faculty to keep abreast of and gain from what is going on in other parts of the world. Their statewide and discipline clientele and the university's status in this global society depend in part on such acquaintance and information exchange.

The global reality of research and expertise is a "two-edged" sword. To what extent does or will the strengths and intellectual capacities of universities around the world affect U.S. universities' research funding? Why should a multinational company that needs university research expertise fund U.S. scientists if they can get equal expertise and research capacity at half the cost elsewhere?

Although I emphasize a global perspective in these chapters, I am reminded that "all politics is local" and that support to the university is exercised via the political process. And, a majority of your university's clients and potential supporters are residents of your state. Although a large proportion of your university's business and professional clientele are in some form of global market and competition, in most cases their offices and their production facilities are *nearby*, within a few miles or a few hundred miles of your campus. Those nearby communities are where most of the university's research and extension *output* will be delivered; it is those communities, as well as individual clientele, that are the immediate beneficiaries.

While I was at SDSU, our board had endorsed our request for new research greenhouses and I had made my pitch—all the details—to the state legislature's joint appropriations committee. I was not sure I had their attention. I was followed by Dick Daley, a wheat producer from near the North Dakota border, and his statement to the committee was brief. "In one of my first farming years it was dry; I didn't raise enough wheat to pay my $300 real estate tax bill. Last year was drier, but I paid $3,000 in real estate taxes and I also paid some income tax. Why?

Because of the drought-resistant lines of wheat SDSU research has developed. *We* need those greenhouses." The money for the greenhouses was endorsed within minutes. (Local and global: Dick Daley lived in South Dakota, but about 60 percent of U.S. wheat is generally exported.)

While drafting this chapter, I had an hour-long visit with a 50-year-old friend who had applied to be a county extension education director (multicounty in some states). He wanted advice. I warned him the county director position was not the same as it was in his father's time or "his own time." (He had been a member of the county extension council 20 years earlier.) As county director, he would be expected to be on a first-name basis with the heads of the local manufacturing businesses, chamber of commerce, community college, school system, and industry organizations, as well as the mayors, city councils, county commissioners, state senator and representatives, 4-H leaders, and a good many individual retailers and professional people. He should be able to link them to any part of the state university that might be useful—and the university to them.

Though the Vice Provost for Extension at the University would "sign-off" on his employment, if endorsed by the area director, the main selection decision would be made by the local, elected county extension council. (He was hired and is doing very well.)

In virtually every state, university technology and professional expertise provided through extension-type programs for start-up companies, to assist with new product development or quality traits, or to assess or refine production or distribution systems could comprise a long list. Seminars, conferences, short courses, individual site visits, and consultation by extension specialists or campus-based research staff have major influence on the economy of the state and individual communities, as well as the financial success of individual businesses and professionals. That impact is "local."

We decry that state appropriations comprise a smaller percent of the typical state university budget, largely the result of increased fund competition from other worthy needs. However, bear in mind that your state university's success in competing with those other needs will be *in proportion* to the degree that statewide clientele and their elected governor and legislators *believe your university is useful* to the economic and social growth of the state, as well as to its college-age students.

At the University of Nebraska, my staff and I developed—after involving about 120 commodity and natural resource organization leaders in setting priorities—an aggressive legislative request for consideration by the board of regents at their November meeting. A dozen of those leaders showed up at that meeting and asked for the privilege to speak in support. The request was unanimously approved.

Why does Congress put research and development money into the National Institutes of Health (NIH), DOE, HHS and other federal agencies? Who provides supporting testimony before the appropriations committees and subcommittees or phone calls, faxes, and e-mails to committee members? Certainly the agencies, themselves, but the most credible and effective support comes from clientele. Seven years ago my wife, and I were in the halls of the National Cancer

Institute (one of the NIHs) with our daughter, son-in-law, and twin grandsons, Clay and Eric. A dermatologist at the University of Iowa Medical College had suggested Clay's persistent skin rash might be a form of cancer. An oncologist at the University of Nebraska Medical Center, Dr. Jim Armitage, had confirmed the diagnosis as an acute and aggressive form of "leukemia-lymphoma." (The then-recently-established cause was a specific virus prevalent in the Caribbean, South Pacific, and Japan.) Prescribed chemotherapy proved more than Clay's body could stand, and the only hope was in on-going NIH research, with which Dr. Armitage was involved. We headed to Bethesda and NIH.

Being identical twins and, as premature births, both recipients of blood transfusions (the likely virus source), and one with the malady symptoms and the other without, they were ideal research subjects and admitted to the NIH research program. Since then Clay has been at the NIH campus perhaps 20 times, Eric at least annually. Both twins, at this writing, are in college.

Professionally, in consulting, the food business, biotechnology, and university research and curriculum issues, my focus is global. But, in terms of the value of those two state university medical centers and the National Institutes of Health, my interest is local. It is our grandsons.

Think globally, act locally. University leadership at all levels—and led by you, the president—should encourage, budget, and seek funds for global interaction and relationships by research and extension faculty, as well as by the instructors (likely, in many cases, the same people) to keep them in tune with and ahead of their global competition. Your management team should then make sure the university's delivery and engagement mechanisms, web sites, publications, licensing, seminars, consultation, conferences, and other forms of technology and knowledge transfer reach those local clientele, the residents, businesses, and communities of your state. Your university's clientele businesses, professions, and state residents will be better competitors in that global economy and global market, more knowledgeable citizens in the global society, and stronger supporters of your university.

Among the mechanisms universities use to focus and link faculty expertise to specific industries, technology sectors, or geographic regions are multidisciplinary institutes and centers. Their value, formation, and operations are discussed in the next chapter.

CHAPTER

Multidiscipline Institutes, Centers and Locations

A university does not need a formal institute or center for the faculty of many disciplines to work together. Acquaintance, recognition of expertise, and goodwill are sufficient. In fact, cooperation is often easier without a formal structure. My advice to deans and department heads has been, "Let your faculty know you expect them to work across department and college lines. Then stay out of the way; do not worry about which unit gets the credit."

Institutes or centers, however, give visibility to an issue and can formally advance a roster of scientists in disciplines from which that issue needs expertise, and they are effective instruments in attracting government, industry, or private funds. An institute or center gives identity and demonstrates focus to an issue the *funder* may want addressed. A funding proposal can list faculty from many disciplines; if the money comes, the project will get the faculties' attention and time.

A wealthy family or a foundation may want to see research focus on hydrogen as an energy source, and have the topic addressed by engineers, physicists, chemists, economists, geneticists (plants are a likely hydrogen source), and any other. A western governor may have proposed, and the state legislature set aside, money to stimulate exports. An East Asia Trade Institute, with faculty from business, political science, and other departments will appear rather quickly at one of the state universities. That rule of my financial consultant friend, "Be poised to pounce," is fitting in universities.

It is the university's collection of diverse disciplines that prompts federal and state agencies, political leaders, and the private sector to turn to the university to address their needs! The university "holds valuable cards;" an institute or center can put "all the right cards in one hand."

Establishment. Your university policy for formation of an institute or center should be clear, both on criteria and approval process. Governing board approval is likely required for an institute; policy may allow presidential approval for centers. Without such clear policy, institutes or centers will sprout, in some cases just to satisfy faculty pride or to "mark out territory." A college or department may want to pre-empt an emerging field of work.

I suggest four principles for establishment:

1. Have a clear reason and stated mission for each.
2. Have a system for approving the establishment.
3. Keep administration simple.
4. Avoid bad compromises or reporting arrangements.

I offer examples of the latter: Both civil engineering and microbiology may feel leadership on municipal water quality is their responsibility, and water is the focus of several federal grant programs. Each department may propose a Center for the Study of Municipal Water Supplies, headquartered in their department; or, Psychology, Human Development, and Adult Education may each assume they are the logical home for a Geriatric Learning Institute you or the provost has proposed. You see potential funding from the Department of Education or the Department of Health and Human Services. In each case, not only two or three departments, but two or three colleges, are involved. Repeated meetings of involved deans and department heads fail to resolve the home base for the proposed institutes or the division of labor. "Let's make these university-wide institutes reporting to the provost's office!"

Probably a bad compromise! So many institutes and centers already report to the provost and associate provost that these two get delegated to an assistant to the associate. That person may or may not have acquaintance with the sectors; more important, he or she has no direct control of any of the facilities or staff that are important to the work. But, no dean or department head has "lost a jurisdictional battle."

A private donor (or an agency) may want "their" unit to report to you, as president. "If it has the president's attention, what we want to happen will happen." A wise president will avoid that; you already have a provost, vice presidents, and deans to support!

Iowa State lists 61 centers, institutes, and other interdepartmental or intercollege entities. Fifteen report to the vice provost for research and the rest to deans or department heads. Deans and department heads not only have high vested interest in those units' success, they have the administrative framework—requisition, payroll, personnel handling, and so on—which an institute may not have. And, Institutes may not have the funds to establish such administrative frame work.

If an institute or center is truly university-wide, involves a major facility used by multiple colleges, and has sufficient funding to provide the administrative infrastructure of accounting and other such functions, reporting to a provost or vice provost may be best. Where such is not the case, however, it should report to the lowest practical level and, in most instances, that level is a dean or a department head. A technique I have used and seen used effectively works like this: If there are several proposed multicollege institutes (or centers, or even curriculums), assign A and B to Dean 1, C and D to Dean 2, etc. If such is done with involvement and subject matter consideration by the several deans, each dean not only carries a fair share of responsibility, but also has some "trading stock." "I'll see to it that your faculty is treated fairly in the institutes I handle if you'll see to it that my faculty is treated fairly in the institutes you handle. If you'll run interference for that institute, I'll run interference for this one." Trading stock among college deans and department heads is as important in universities as it is among companies in the private sector or federal agencies; it helps in getting things done and issues resolved.

You and your provost also may also suggest that each dean will be evaluated in part according to the degree of multiple-discipline contribution to the success of institutes for which he or she carries leadership responsibility.

Center and institute clientele. While the funders, or deans and department heads, may be concerned about program identity and about where such a unit reports, most clientele—users of the knowledge that may pour out—could not care less! They go to the *person*, the one they believe has the expertise they need.

When the combining of that small poultry science department with the larger animal science department at SDSU was announced, I was concerned some industry leaders might be distressed (even though I had taken most of the steps listed in Chapter 27). We had just received appropriations for new poultry facilities, thanks largely to the industry's political support. A few days after we announced the consolidation, I met several industry leaders outside my office to go visit the construction site. As soon as I got in the car, I mentioned the department consolidation, figuring I just as well take any heat right away. *They changed the subject!* Organization was my problem! The scientists they respected were still on board, I had made a commitment of continued budget allocation, and the industry would have the research they wanted from those new facilities.

Multi-discipline, off-Campus facilities. Your university may have an office or facility in one of the state's major metropolitan areas. It may offer night classes in engineering, education, and business and it may house an urban forester, a nutrition education program for low-income families, an economist working with retailers, and a research project focused on urban youth. Or, in a distant corner of the state, you may have a university center that includes an industrial engineer working with small manufacturers, an economic development specialist, an area horticulturist, a research/extension agronomist, and a supervisor of the area's county extension offices. How does one mesh the need for some program coordination in the geographic area with (also needed) discipline program coordination? To whom do those staff members report? Who recommends salary increases, promotions, and, in some cases, tenure? And, there are some mundane but sensitive issues, such as office hours, leave time, letterhead, or how phones are answered. These need to be decided, but by whom?

With SDSU at the east end of the state, we established a West River agricultural research and extension center in Rapid City, relocated several live-stock, range management, and crops research and extension people to that site, and named a senior member of the group as "center director." Rapid City is the trading center for the region and clientele needs are far different from those of eastern South Dakota. I wanted the center staff to be reading the *Rapid City Gazette* and the *Rocky Mountain News* instead of the *Sioux Falls Argus Leader* or the *Minneapolis Tribune*, and tuning to the same radio and TV stations as their clientele. They needed to be in tune with their region. They also needed to know and work with West River political and industry leadership.

At the same time, each faculty member needed to be a meaningful part of their subject matter department. Each needed to interact and coordinate programs with their professional colleagues and subject matter department heads. Further, each faculty member's professional future lay in that subject matter discipline.

A colleague loaned me a well-worn book written by an official of the WWII Office of Price Administration (OPA), a citation I cannot now locate. That agency had national price and rationing criteria, policy, and reporting structure by commodity—tires vs. gasoline vs. sugar vs. butter, for example. It also had a regional structure for personnel policies, delivery of ration stamps, and handling appeals or special problems. The author paralleled that agency with General Motors, which had and still has a product structure—parts vs. service vs. Cadillac vs. Buick—and a geographic structure (regional offices) to work with dealers on store operations, area advertising, and financing.

One administrative structure, in such a situation, is usually supreme, with decision prerogative for program direction, personnel, and budget. When a busi-ness or agency administers largely by product line, staff dedicated to geographic issues complain about lack of attention or input. After years of hearing such com-plaints, the CEO may reverse the supremacy in decision prerogative. Soon, the product people complain.

The moral of the book was to *acknowledge the necessity* of both administrative structures and that the two sets of supervisory officers need to talk a lot, keep each other posted. Major decisions, such as promotions, salary, or when and how to initiate a new program, can then be more easily negotiated. Regardless of whether the discipline administrator or the regional administrator takes the lead-ership role on a specific issue, the opposite can more comfortably provide needed input and support.

For that West River Center, I told the center director and the subject depart-ment heads I would appraise their work, in part, by the number of times they talked by phone. When promotion and salary recommendations came in from each department head, I wanted each one endorsed (perhaps after negotiation) by the center director. And, each year those department heads and I spent a day together at the Rapid City office reviewing the total West River program with the center director and staff.

This concept is applicable to major multidiscipline institutes or centers where discipline faculty may devote all or a major portion of their time. Who has the supreme prerogative in salary and promotions, the discipline department head/dean or the institute director? Should either? The two need to talk a lot!

Joint ventures with other agencies or universities. In a recent Iowa State extension staff conference, I encountered serious concern from those involved in joint educational ventures with community colleges, state agencies, and other groups. "How do we retain our identity? How does Iowa State receive its credit?"

There may be a Regents Center, with staff from several state universities, or some university staff may be housed in a state agency or a community college. Do the clientele in that area recognize that the faculty located there are a part of your university? Or, does your university lose some "public exposure" benefit in student recruitment and political support? This is not something I have been concerned about over the years, believing that clientele know who does the good work and that appropriate credit will come. However, what I heard in that conference were repeated, sincere, and well-illustrated concerns.

Several guidelines came from the ensuing discussion: (1) See that the quality of every presentation, visual, or publication, and university staff's professional manner, exceed those of others. (2) Have visible university logos on shirts, sports jackets, caps, and/or any university autos, as well as on publications and other visuals. (3) For jointly prepared brochures or other physical and visual material, have negotiated and written policies regarding use of each involved entities' names and logos.

Although clientele usually do know who is doing the work and where credit belongs, such guidelines and practices can avoid some conflicts and concerns. The discussion reminded me: The staff members were concerned because they were very proud of their university! As president, that is what you want.

Another effective mechanism to facilitate technology transfer from the university to the private sector is an adjacent or nearby research park, a subject tackled in Chapter 33.

CHAPTER

Research Parks

I f your state university does not have a research park or an "incubator" where new technology and ideas from faculty research can be developed or linked with the private sector, you will likely consider one. If it does have a research park, there will be some problems and issues in which you (and the provost and, at least, some deans and department heads) will be involved. A research park is another way that your state university can play its expected role in the state's economic development. With continuing economic pressures, demographic changes, and global competition in all sectors, governors and legislators look increasingly to their state universities for concepts, inventions, processes, and products that might spark economic growth.

Des Moines Register columnist David Yepsen recently discussed the marching orders Governor Tom Vilsack had given his new appointees to the Iowa Board of Regents.[21] He quoted the governor, in part, "From an economic development standpoint, the regents have a very important role. First, they have to create a climate of entrepreneurship . . . They have to continue to revise the rewards they have for faculty. In the past it's been publish a paper, write a book, and you get rewarded. Well, now it's come up with an idea, start a business and you'll get rewarded."

Governing boards and governors certainly recognize broader missions of state universities than these quotes imply, but such expressions are not unique to Iowa. Leaders and taxpayers in every state expect university talent and technology to find or develop practical and functional outlets—beyond publications, workshops, and conferences—for commercialization of technology and "intellectual property." From that, they anticipate state economic growth and societal benefit.

A research park—land, buildings, and equipment—where faculty can, independently or in partnership with venture investors or established businesses, develop pilot models or modest production operations is one of those outlets. The North Carolina Research Triangle is the recognized model, and has the good fortune to be located among three major research universities, the University of North Carolina, North Carolina State University, and Duke University.

An existing university research park may have been initiated by the university, its foundation, a local business group, or the state. Initial enthusiasm likely brought external funds, perhaps for land, a building or two, and maybe some major equipment. Several million state dollars may have been provided. Facilities are likely leased at a modest, perhaps subsidized, rate to faculty or faculty/business partners.

I recently spent part of an afternoon with Iowa State Research Park Director, Steve Carter, discussing some of a park's features, issues, and problems. And, I have watched university research parks from several perspectives. The output of some of our USDA scientists, based on university campuses and working in cooperation with university faculty, was further developed and commercialized in university research parks. Some of the funds of an investment corporation I chaired are in a biotech company now leasing space in Iowa State's park. I have watched that park grow and new buildings being added over the past decade. Among 50 or so tenants in the Iowa State park, about half began as joint efforts by faculty and an established business. A few were initiated by nonuniversity technology companies, each seeking proximity to faculty expertise related to its core business. The others were initiated by individual faculty, faculty teams, or faculty–student teams.

Most university faculty with a product or concept they believe—or someone else believes—has market potential lack start-up money, and they also lack private sector production, marketing, or financing experience. They dig into savings, borrow, and/or find investment partners. Or, they set out to locate a going business with interest in their idea or product and negotiate some form of ownership and operating agreement. But, they have no experience in negotiating such agreements!

Can your university's College of Business help? Perhaps, but a college of business may or may not be "entrepreneurial." In some, the faculty and curriculum focus is corporate employment, or providing accounting or consulting services to corporations. In contrast, Carter mentioned, most veterinarians expect to start, buy, or partner in a private business. Iowa State chose to combine the research park directorship with that of its Pappajohn Entrepreneurship Center, the latter established to foster entrepreneurship among faculty and students of all colleges. (Iowa State now offers a university-wide undergraduate minor in entrepreneurship.) Carter is director of both the Park and the Center, so he and his staff can easily work with faculty on the several issues needed for Park occupants' success.

What are the continuing problems? To quote Carter, "We're always walking the line between the university community and the business community. My staff and I need to 'talk the talk' of both and, with some difficulty, operate by the rules of both."

I have seen that from an investment perspective. A business mind focuses first on getting a good product into the market ahead of competition. The next focus is getting volume product out the door at minimum cost and cash in the door, for both cash flow and profit. The academic mind is intrigued by a product's features and may continue tweaking toward perfection. But, to "make a business," one must *produce and sell*. Venture capitalists may say it another way, "Creative people start ventures; managers make ventures profitable." It is rare for a person to be both.

How about university rights to or partial interests in patents, copyrights, or a resultant company's profits? In what cases should there be joint agreements, licensing, and cost and revenue sharing among the university (or its research park entity), the faculty member, and a partner business? There is no universal answer, except that any circumstance can be negotiated.

Is there an end point for a research park? Is it perpetual? Should the university continue to "sponsor" or subsidize? When the new wears off and state or local community subsidies are exhausted, can it continue with subsidized rental rates and supporting services? Should successful and "graduate" businesses be committed to return a portion of their largesse to the park for its continued operation? Should a research park eventually become a private enterprise, just another specialized real estate development? Or, should it continue as a nonprofit quasi-university, quasi-city, or quasi-state entity? If one of the latter, can it carry itself financially, or will it be subsidized by the university or its foundation? Can you, the university leadership, convince the host city or county to reinvest (it can mean potential tax revenue)? Or will a state department of economic development see the need and subsidize the project?

If your state university is to fully and continuously play the economic development role, the merits of a research park will be the same in the next decade as in this. And, the faculty members with the next ideas, concepts, or products with commercial potential will have the same voids—capital, production experience, sales experience, and financing experience. The same subsidization will likely be needed. And, money will be needed for maintenance and upgrades of the research park facilities, the facilities those early tenants used.

If your university does not have a research park, are there other issues to consider? It costs money to start one. It needs a clear focus, perhaps limited to technology, perhaps broad, but clear to all. It should enhance entrepreneurial interests, attitudes, and skills among both faculty and students. It should, when in operation, provide some student employment and exposure to the private sector.

One might parallel a research park with intercollegiate athletics. Both present problems. But, if your university did not have an athletics program, you would likely start one to build university enthusiasm and public identity. If your state university does not have a research park, you, with encouragement from a couple of deans or departments, will likely consider starting one to help get university technology and concepts implemented into business and society.

No part of any state university is more involved in daily transfer of technology, science, and skill to an appreciative clientele and no part of a state university presents more financial and management challenges than what is discussed in the next chapter—Medical Schools and Teaching Hospitals.

CHAPTER 34

Medical Schools and
Teaching Hospitals

I
f the university that you aspire to head or have been chosen to head has no
medical school, you can skip this chapter. If there is a medical school and if you
come to the presidency role from having been the chief administrator of a university medical center, then too you can skip this chapter. If, however, you are likely to
be responsible for a medical school and come without such experience, having had
experience most likely as a provost, vice president, and/or dean of another college,
perhaps from a university without a college of medicine, as I would, I offer several
suggestions. Obtain and read the latest version of *The Handbook of Academic
Medicine* published by the Association of American Medical Colleges, Washington,
D.C.[22] It will give you a basic understanding of how medical schools and teaching
hospitals work. Then find a university medical center administrator, or one who
has till recently been one, who is willing to spend time listing and discussing major
issues a state university president can expect to face.

Dr. David Smith, Chancellor of the Texas Tech University System and former
President of the Texas Tech Health Sciences Center, was most generous in giving
me a "short course" on key issues as I drafted this chapter, and several state university trustees from whom I sought input were helpful with their perspectives.

In the interview with the university governing board, you should get a reading
on board members' understanding of the medical school and related hospital
issues. Is there, for example, a board committee that devotes attention to this
area? Does the board or that committee know the legal or contract structures? Do
they know the financial issues? What are the board's expectations?

The chapters in Part II, The Knowledge Base, described much of the knowledge that you, as a new president, will need and want. In the case of a medical center, there is more:

1. What curriculums are included in the college or center? Is it limited to the M.D. degree or are there programs for physicians' assistants, nurse practitioners, nursing, pharmacy, physical therapy, or other?
2. Is there a university teaching hospital and is it managed by the university? Or does the college contract with other hospitals, private or public, for teaching and clinical experience? What are the major features of these agreements?
3. What is the budget structure? Are there separate units—college, hospital, clinics, institutes—and budgets? What are the income sources, expenditure categories, and trends?
4. How are the clinic faculty practice plans structured? Are they inside—a part of the university—or are they in a legal structure outside the university? What are the contractual relationships? What policy board guides these?
5. What do the governor, key legislators, and people of the state see as the major need and expectation of the medical center?
6. How is the M.D. (or other) curriculum structured, and how recently has it been revised?

From the several people with whom you, as a prospective or new president will consult, a list will develop of the major medical center issues, in order of priority, and some of these will need your, and perhaps the board's, attention. In many respects, those issues and problems that a medical college and teaching hospital face parallel those of the balance of the university; they just tend to be more intense and more complex. Constant flow of new medical knowledge, procedures, and equipment and competition for faculty means greater costs. More health professionals need to be trained and the people want and need convenient health service sites. These come at a cost. At the same time, many people lack health insurance coverage, charity cases increase, there are limits on Medicare reimbursement, and state appropriations are generally level.

Smith calls it "the perfect storm." He characterizes a medical center's status, with the pressures for more training and more service but with multiple state regulations and constraints, as "moving from state-supported to state-assisted to state-molested!"

To keep the curriculum current and to graduate professionals in reasonable time, almost continual review is needed. New subject matter requires sorting of what is to be included vs. what is to be forgone. Changes in the medical delivery system—more care delivery in community-based clinics, more out-patient surgery, and shorter hospital stays—mean the students need to spend time in more places to see the spectrum of illnesses and treatment.

The time clinical faculty must devote to practice in order to obtain the income needed to support the academic programs limits their academic time.

If the university contracts for management of the university hospital, or with other hospitals for teaching sites, pass-through of any Medicare or other funds to help finance the academic programs has to be negotiated. Both the hospital management and the university need the money.

Most research funding comes from the National Institutes of Health and a few other agencies, nearly all in the form of competitive grants or contracts. Overhead cost recovery is limited and often inadequate in meeting real overhead costs. Private research funds focus generally on drugs or procedures with market potential.

In terms of a medical center and teaching hospital, what should be your major foci and perhaps those of a provost? From Smith's observations and those of others, here are items that should be high on your list:

1. See that programs are accountable to the state's needs—training of physicians and other professionals, relationships to and support of local trauma centers and hospitals—to the extent that funds allow.
2. Articulate to all audiences the accountability, the extent of the center's services and value of that medical center to the state's citizenry.
3. Lobby the governor and state director of Medicaid administration for an adequate "set-aside" or allocation to medical education. The allocation will vary among states and will depend on Medicaid dollars received, characteristics of the state's population, and the center's demonstrated needs and services.
4. Highlight medical center capital and program needs in private fund-raising. Health care and medical facilities are "front and center" in the minds of many. To give to such a noble cause has infinite appeal to some with large financial resources.
5. Encourage and facilitate linkages between health sciences faculty and those in economics, social sciences, psychology, the biological and physical sciences, statistics, and other disciplines. It is from multidisciplinary synergy that some needed concepts in health maintenance, care, care delivery, and treatment may come.
6. Keep the university governing board informed of both the problems and the achievements in the health sciences. Build their awareness and acquaintance with the budget and program issues. Do the same with the governor (or at least one of the governor's key staff) and key legislators.

Health care policy and medical funding is largely federal. Any adjustments in that federal part—dollars, legislation, or regulations regarding NIH, Medicare, Medicaid, and research policy—will have significant impact on a medical center. The more the governing board members (and governor and key legislators) know and understand, the better able they will be to respond when their action is needed. That also says, "Keep the state's Congressional delegation informed."

You need to spend some time in the Medical Center and out-state or off-campus facilities; you need to be there often enough so that staff and students know that you know about and care about their work and their issues. As with others of your management team, you need to take time to express thanks to medical center department heads and other administrators for their leadership and their efforts. With such complex issues, not everyone who is capable of being an administrator wants to be.

CHAPTER 35

Councils and Committees

One of the largest favors a departing president can do for a successor is to send a letter of thanks to members of administrative and advisory councils, thanking them for their service and advice and including a phrase such as, "the new president should have the privilege of structuring administrative and advisory councils and their functions for the years ahead." If that has not happened, I suggest you announce early that thought is being given to such councils and to how they will be structured "for most value at this stage in the university's development." You may choose the same council names and same structures as had existed, but I would urge some change. Each needs to be *your* council.

What councils are needed? You can study the council structures on the websites of comparable universities and consider a variety of options. The university or faculty handbook may list certain president's councils and their functions. You should not consider yourself locked in; that handbook can be revised.

Were I a new president, I would start with an administrative council that would include, as a minimum, the provost, vice presidents, and deans. Whatever the title, your top university information officer, your media link and support should be a member. Next, I would likely want some form of internal, university-wide advisory and communication council that would include elected faculty, non-faculty staff, and student leadership. Or, depending on circumstances, I may prefer three separate advisory groups. Should deans be members of these latter councils? Perhaps one or two, for "a dean's perspective" on issues.

I would not rush this task of forming advisory councils. I would take it a step at a time, starting with the people and positions I knew I wanted; I can add. I would not make an announcement that "this is my administrative council" until I felt comfortable doing so. Some presidents have what they call an "executive council," such as the CEO–COO–CFO–CMO central group of top officers suggested in Chapter 13. Of course, one can counsel with these people without having a formal group name!

In my successive administrative positions, there has been variation in how well my close associates interacted. In one case, two personalities clashed enough that group discussions were usually of limited value. Each would give me valuable counsel, but I would generally consult with each individually. Only when an issue was very compelling and urgent did we benefit from a group session.

In some universities, there is a Dean's Council that elects its chair from among the deans. Such may have merit in some cases, but it certainly conveys the impression that deans are not part of the president's central administrative team. Far more logical is a council of deans either chaired by the provost, representing the president, or with the president as chair and the provost as vice chair.

How about an external advisory council? As president, you already have the governing board, the alumni association board, and, probably, a foundation board. And each college may have an advisory council. However, some presidents establish a rather large external advisory council in order to formally include key people they simply want to tap for advice and for communication in the opposite and outward direction, to spread the word about the university and its needs. If you form such a group, or if such already exists, I suggest you include among the members the chair or a couple of members from each college advisory council.

Every presidential council takes presidential time. The members of the council need to meet often enough for them to feel their involvement is meaningful and that they are, in fact, useful to the president. I suggest you structure council work according to the university's needs—and competitive needs for your time.

Standing committees and councils. Perhaps the most significant university body within this general heading—and of most importance to both a president and the faculty in resolving major university issues—is the faculty senate (or comparable body).

Early in my faculty years at Iowa State, I found myself as chair of the then-Iowa State College Faculty Council. It was the forerunner of an eventual faculty senate and comprised one elected person of each faculty rank from each of the five colleges. On a Sunday morning near the end of the legislative session, President Hilton called, "Can you get the Faculty Council together in my conference room at 11 o'clock? I need some input from the Council."

When we were gathered and seated, Hilton explained, "It appears we can get the votes in the state legislature to change the College's formal and legal name from Iowa State College of Agriculture and Mechanic Arts to Iowa State University of Science and Technology. I would feel a lot more comfortable if this were discussed by the Council and, if you agree, to have your formal support of the change on behalf of the faculty." Though a few may have had traditional reverence for "agriculture and mechanic arts" as part of the title, "Science and Technology" to follow "Iowa State University of" was certainly apt. Discussion was brief; a motion of support was made, seconded, and unanimously passed.

Most universities have a long list of other councils and committees: each should fill a need for policy development, coordination, and/or communication. There is likely an elected faculty senate and appointed or elected councils or major committees for intercollegiate athletics, library resources, laboratory animal welfare, human subjects research, capital improvements, safety, space assignment, and other. For some, membership—and their duties and prerogatives—may be prescribed in a faculty handbook or other document. For those roles that you consider major, it is worthwhile to note their duties and prerogatives.

Within days of my arrival as president, a committee my predecessor had named recommended that the athletic director no longer report to the Athletic Council but, instead, directly to the president. There was also a "minority report" from a couple of members disagreeing with that recommendation. I consulted with my vice presidents and approved the majority recommendation. Big mistake! The change not only removed some insulation valuable to me in a sector sure to bring some problems, but it diminished the role and strength of the council!

Among the most important committees or councils are those related to curriculum, academic advising, student recruitment, research coordination, and state-wide extension programs. For a university curriculum committee, I would urge that each of the college committee chairs be a member. That insures that all related information is available on any issue; the committee can then be more efficient.

I would review the committee and council list to see if there are any additions or changes needed to bring focus and faculty input to my major goals or charges given me by the board. Are there parts of a strategic plan that need committee attention? Is an accreditation review in the offing? And are there redundant committees? Some may be standing committees, continuing year after year, perhaps with rotating membership named by the administration, with recommendations from colleges or other units or from a faculty senate committee on committees.

Search–and–screening committees. Appointing such for a central administrative post or a deanship may be one of your first tasks. It is important to review university policies and any established guidelines for such; some universities have a detailed prescribed plan to insure thoroughness and consistency in every such search. You will likely need to follow them, but I have seen some that are unduly burdensome. I would not let such guidelines keep me from proceeding with dispatch.

When I named a screening committee for a central officer or dean position, I made clear their task was to identify and attract high-quality candidates and nominees and to narrow the group to approximately six that the committee felt were highly qualified. Those six or so names were not to be ranked, and I gave my reasons:

1. I would do some more checking on each; there was a chance I would learn positives or negatives that the committee had not learned.
2. I wanted the prerogative to insure, among the finalists interviewed, that the person chosen could work effectively with me and my provost.
3. Were my eventual choice different from the committee's first ranked, committee members may feel their advice had been ignored. That would not be constructive.

4. Were the person appointed not first on the committee's ranked list, there may be a perception we had "settled for second or third choice." That would not be constructive either.

I also made clear that after receiving the names, reviewing their materials and, perhaps, making a few of our own phone calls, the provost and I would meet with the committee to listen to members' oral comments, positives and negatives, about each. After an hour or so of that discussion, the provost and I would leave the meeting rather confident regarding which and how many among the finalists had greater committee regard.

Such search-and-screening committees nearly always do their jobs well, but I have seen some rare exceptions. In one case, an obviously well qualified person was left off the shortlist because "the committee felt he was too strong and competitive in his current post." What committee members ignored was that he would be similarly "strong and competitive" in that new post! (We apparently had some of the wrong people on that committee.)

I am aware of another case on a campus where I was not directly involved: A committee charged with providing a list "from diverse and representative disciplines" wanted to avoid the appointing authority naming a person from a certain discipline. They therefore chose who they thought was a less acceptable person to represent, on their list, that "discipline spot." You guessed it! That was the person the appointing authority chose! Such may be among the issues discussed with a committee when they are appointed and charged.

Ad-hoc committees. When confronted with a contentious or emotional issue, the safest route for a president—or perhaps a provost or dean—is to name a committee. Committee proceedings give needed time for all issues to emerge and be understood. It may also allow emotions to subside before a final judgment is made. An ad-hoc committee can be especially helpful to a president in the case of alleged impropriety by an administrator, faculty, or staff member. Such a committee can give broad input, thorough discussion of the key elements, and a recommendation or a number of options to consider.

The same is true for significant organizational issues. Chapter 26 describes a major personnel and structural problem at Kansas State for which I named an ad-hoc faculty/industry/student committee to advise me. There had been undue turmoil and threats of legal action. The solution had to be one that would be "accepted by all." In looking back on that process, I am convinced that a critical factor in the acceptance of the solution decided upon by faculty, clientele, *and the individual personnel involved* was the respect for and credibility of those chosen for the committee.

As appointments are made to committees, I urge that you, the provost, dean or other appointing body give special attention to diversity of membership, racial/ethnic, men vs. women, and among the faculty or staff ranks. It is important that committees have broad and open input and that on every important issue diverse perspectives be offered and considered. It is especially important to include some of the younger faculty. As the tabular data in Chapter 9 indicate, younger faculty and faculty of the lower ranks will more likely be women and ethnic minorities and their proportions will more likely parallel those of the student body, your university's major clientele. Committee work is an opportunity for young, able faculty to become acquainted with faculty of other colleges and with university-wide issues. They will gain needed experience, and they can be "sized up" for future leadership and administrative roles.

CHAPTER

The Athletics Business

On the eve of my assuming the Kansas State presidency, I was invited by retiring President James McCain to a meeting of the university foundation executive committee. On arrival, I learned the agenda was a proposed loan to the athletics department to pay some of the previous fall's football team charter flight, bus bills, and visiting team guarantees. I knew Kansas State was on probation for football recruiting violations and had changed coaches. But now, unpaid bills! I said to myself, "What did I get into?" And, there was more.

After the full problem had been laid out to the executive committee and a moment of stunned silence, banker member Al Hostetler, whom I would learn to appreciate for his common sense and loyalty, spoke, "But, the foundation already has three loans to the department that aren't current!"

In the end, the executive committee decided they had no choice; they approved the loan. But, they added several conditions, including that the chair of the athletic council (who was not at the meeting) co-sign the note and that the athletic department bring current the payments on the other loans. From what I had heard, a council chair would be foolish to co-sign a note and the latter—bringing current other loan payments—would be impossible.

With that new loan those overdue bills got paid, but in terms of athletics I would have no honeymoon. Within days I was to learn, after some digging by my finance staff, that the department had a $500,000 negative net worth as well as a relatively new athletic dormitory, already in bad physical condition and losing about $100,000 per year. A couple of minor sports had been dropped and some students recruited for those sports had been left hanging without the sport or their scholarships.

Athletics is a potent university-marketing device. It can build student and staff enthusiasm, enhance university loyalty, and attract new students and donors.

It gives the university column inches in major papers and time on TV and radio. Athletics is especially appreciated by local businesses; big crowds spend a lot of money for meals, motels, gasoline, and general shopping.

A strong program in any sport, but especially in football and basketball, will attract into the university family some people with no previous connection to the institution. Michener's *Sports in America*[23] describes well this phenomenon as well as other very positive features of athletics.

At the same time, those supporters, with the wrong kind of encouragement—or silence—from coaches or athletic directors can get a program into difficulty with the NCAA or conference rules. Most coaches try hard to understand and live by the rules. And most highly recruited players also know the rules. If they should be recruited improperly they can "blow the whistle" on a coach at any time. A good, thinking coach will not give a player that option!

It is usually a coach under intense pressure or a naïve or overenthusiastic supporter who causes the problems. However, there have also been cases of carelessness or complicity by an admissions or registrar's office, with pressure from coaches or even from higher administration.

The bright spots in our men's athletics program on my arrival were basketball and track. DeLoss Dodds, later to become Athletics Director (AD) at Kansas State and, later still, at the University of Texas, was running an excellent track program, and men's basketball coach Jack Hartman would consistently take the modest talent he could recruit with limited budget to contention for the conference championship.

At least half of the successful college coaches—and some that are not so successful—might be described by some as "prima donnas." The successful ones no doubt have a right to be. They are in the entertainment business, idolized by youth, sought by fans and donors for close friendship, and wildly cheered by students. They are in a "heady world," and sometimes trap themselves into events that require president's time and try their souls.

Apparently distressed by several things, including my reticence to quickly endorse the "need" and start a fund drive for a new basketball arena (to replace a 25-year-old field house) and piqued by some decisions of our new AD, Jersey Jermeier, Hartman resigned at season's end, my second year, to return to his alma mater, Oklahoma State, as coach. By the next night, though, my athletic council chair, Professor Bob Snell, called to tell me Hartman was back in town. He had arrived in Stillwater to the reality that Oklahoma State's Gallagher Hall was older and smaller than the field house he had left! He was back in his "former" Kansas State field house office and wanted his job back.

In Hartman's 36-hour absence, students and local fans had wasted no time in letting our popular assistant coach—and me—know that they wanted him to be the new head coach. In fact, while Hartman was on his way back to Kansas State, the fans were holding a rally at the assistant coach's home.

Though Hartman's resignation had included a couple of jabs at "the administration," could I afford to say "no" to the reinstatement of a popular and winning coach? What about the assistant, already thinking he would be head coach next season? What about Oklahoma State, which had hired a coach in good faith and did not know he had left town after their welcoming press conference?

The outcome? By late morning the following day (for which we had scheduled the college plane to take my wife and me to Minneapolis for our women's postseason tournament game and to have our twenty-fifth wedding anniversary dinner there with our daughter and son-in-law), Hartman had made peace with Oklahoma State and Jermeier, had acknowledged our field house was adequate and had committed to "henceforth say some positive things about the university administration." At one o'clock, a quickly assembled pep band accompanied Hartman, Jermeier, and me to a press conference where Hartman came through with a perfect explanation, "Folks, I committed a turnover!"

While our women's team was performing well that afternoon in Minneapolis, with Vice-President Peters and his wife substituting for us in the bleachers, I was making phone calls to some key alumni and boosters to assure them we still had our winning coach. My wife and I then took a late afternoon drive through the Kansas Flint Hills. Coming back through Manhattan, we picked up a couple hamburgers and milk shakes at McDonalds and had our twenty-fifth anniversary dinner in a parking area overlooking Tuttle Creek Lake.

We did lose that assistant coach.

Intercollegiate athletics is a business. Management is mostly about money, coaches, and talent. Regardless of university size, football and men's and women's basketball are the major income sources (except in some northern state universities, where hockey may be king). They help finance the rest of the sports. Major football universities will net $2 to $3 million or more at a home football game. Their home game gross, from ticket sales and concessions, is enough to attract, in preseason, competition from any of the lesser-power teams they want. Those lesser-power teams will likely net more dollars from their guarantee at Florida, Penn State, other major football power than they would playing at home. For that reason, most of the NCAA Division IA universities will have more preconference games at home than on the road.

Bowl games are another source of major income as well as deserved recognition for an outstanding season. Because team selection for bowl competition, at this writing, puts higher emphasis on the win–loss record and lesser emphasis on the strength of the season's opponents, even more of the NCAA Division IA preseason schedules involve lesser-power teams. Traditional bowl contenders would demand home-and-home agreements. Football scheduling is mostly about money.

To a new university president, I offer this advice:

1. Get a complete financial statement from the department of athletics for the two previous years, including income and outgoings, beginning and year-end balances, and showing assets, liabilities, and net worth. Get the signature of the director of athletics and the director of the university foundation (and any other related entity) that the statement represents all funds expended on behalf of or available for the benefit of the department, athletes, or coaches. Review that material for completeness and clarity with the vice president for finance, director of athletics, and chair of the athletic council.

2. Do not depend on just an auditor's report! An audit is dependent on documents provided by the management. Where violations may occur, no documents likely exist. Ask questions. In my first session with the auditor for our department, I asked a question regarding expenditures and got the response, "Do you really want to know?" I had to say "YES" three times before the auditor gave me the answer. And the answer was not good.
3. Review athletic director and coach contracts. Many include rewards for win–loss records, conference championships, postseason competition, and/or academic performance of student athletes. Do they include a penalty or termination clause for patterns of conference or other violations, or violations of university policy? They should.
4. Make clear the goals and expectations for the program, staff, and supporters. Let supporters know those coach contract terms and any new policies, especially the part about termination for patterns of rule violation.
5. Be sure prospective coaches and assistant coaches are checked out thoroughly. Have they ever been involved in recruiting or other violations? If so, why should the university and you, as president, take the risk?
6. Have a strong athletic council and make use of it. A president cannot abdicate responsibility, but the council can give a president both insulation and well-considered recommendations.

My presidential posture regarding intercollegiate athletics was expressed in three points:

1. Follow the rules. Although rule violations may be—and often are—initiated by external parties, if there is a pattern of rule violation, regardless of source, the coach should be terminated. If there is a pattern of *repeated or continued* rule violations, the athletic director should be terminated.
2. Balance the checkbook. Insure complete financial accountability by department management.
3. Expectation: to be in the top half of the conference in every sport and compete for conference championship in two or three.

Many fans want very much to be, and be known as, a friend of the coach. They will do about anything to achieve that friendship, including help in signing that outstanding recruit or keeping a valued player content, sometimes against the rules and telling the coach, "No need for you to know the details!" However, for program integrity, the "I had no knowledge" or "I was not involved" by a coach or athletic director *does not protect the coach's or AD's job!* If the contract terms and university policy include termination for *any pattern* of rule violation *and supporters know it,* they will not want to take the risk. They will find other, proper, ways to befriend the coach.

What was the outcome of Kansas State's debt, probations, and my posture toward financial management and rule violations in athletics? Unfortunately, it was only after another NCAA probation (from a pattern of football violations and resulting in another change in coaches and the AD) that some staff and supporters were willing to hear and believe Numbers 1 and 2 of my posture. In that process, we had some friends of departing coaches and athletic directors who were very unhappy and some busy sports reporters and columnists.

The athletic dorm was transferred to and renovated by the Department of Residence, and athletes were dispersed among housing accommodations with other students. Only a training table was maintained. Kansas State's football team was invited to participate in a bowl game for the first time in 85 years, the credit for that going to Coach Jim Dickey and AD Dick Towers.

After that NCAA probation, there were no significant rule violations (Posture Number1). Debts were paid and the books balanced (Posture Number 2). How about Number 3, team performance? We did not make the top half of the conference (including meets and tournaments) in every sport every year, but I believe that in every sport our coaches and athletes made it some years. In basketball and track, Kansas State was consistently in the top half and we had a reasonable share of conference and conference tournament and meet championships.

Emotion is not absent in any sector of your presidential management responsibilities, but its intensity varies. If athletics is at one end of the "emotion scale," the physical campus, the topic of the next chapter, is probably at the other end. However, for staff and student comfort and pride, management of the physical campus is equally important.

CHAPTER 37

The Physical Campus

Several thousand students, faculty, and staff will go to work almost every morning on your campus. The surroundings through which they walk—the green grass, flowers, and trimmed shrubbery—and the buildings they enter, with welcoming entrances, polished floors, and comfortable offices and classrooms, can have a positive impact. They should go to work inspired and ready to inspire others.

What they see as they move to their workday sends a message about the work they will be doing: A quality environment deserves quality work. Prospective students, their parents, and visiting clientele get the same message: This is a quality university! A well-tended campus suggests well-tended programs. What transpires in the classrooms, faculty offices, and laboratories will be good work.

An adequate maintenance budget plus good facility management is important, but every person can contribute to cleanliness and neatness. As president, you need to acknowledge campus care, express appreciation, and perhaps serve as a model in your daily routine. SDSU President Briggs rarely walked across campus without picking up a gum wrapper or the remnants of a wind-blown newspaper, and I picked up the habit. That campus was where I worked; I wanted to be proud of my workplace, in all respects.

Probably no one on our Kansas State campus appreciated the physical plant staff more than did my wife. Redecoration of the president's home was not yet finished when we arrived, so my wife, eager to get settled and ready for entertaining, donned jeans and spent several days sanding, painting, and varnishing alongside the crew. When it was all finished, including some plantings, she insisted that our first open house would be for all those workers and their families.

For what seemed a steady flow of events at the president's home, staff always had the shrubs trimmed or the drives and walks cleared of snow. In reference to her size, 4' 11" and barely 100 pounds, the word at the staff shop apparently became "We'll get that done for 'Big Mama.'" She was not supposed to know but found out through a student helper and appreciated the endearing humor. Our last week in the presidency, she called the shop to ask if someone would drive their grounds cart down and give her and some cookies she had made a ride up to join them for coffee. It was all she could do to resist putting a note on the cookie tray, "With appreciation, from Big Mama."

Buildings and equipment need not be new to be clean and well maintained. I once toured the facilities of a world-renowned professor of forestry at Purdue University. It was an attic, where graduate students routinely stepped over frame superstructure to access equipment far from new. However, the area was clean and air conditioned, and the equipment appeared well maintained. I asked the professor how his group of technicians and graduate students could be so productive in limited facilities and with rather dated equipment. He responded simply, "The issue is not how new the equipment is; it is how well-maintained it is and whether you calibrate it before you use it." Though state-of-the-art computers, projectors, or electronic assay equipment is certainly preferred, top-flight maintenance is essential.

You may be pressured to take money from the physical plant budget for other pressing needs, delay some repairs and maintenance, skip the flowers at the campus entrance or forego watering the grass on central campus. Do not succumb. Quality surroundings inspire and suggest quality work. It is also a significant source of university—faculty, student, and clientele—pride.

And choose a physical plant manager as carefully as you choose a dean.

CHAPTER

Academic Freedom and Free Speech

A good friend in my early years at both Iowa State and Kansas State was Dr. Adrian Daane, who served a time as head of Kansas State's Chemistry department. Adrian's father had been head of Agronomy at Oklahoma A & M (now Oklahoma State University) and had been fired as part of a "political purge" in 1928.[24] The undocumented but often told story is that the root of the purging was Governor William H. "Alfalfa Bill" Murray's displeasure that the agronomy department was doing research on inorganic fertilizer and presenting that research at farmer meetings. College and university purges or firings were not uncommon in the first half of the twentieth century, before tenure was accepted as policy by some university governing boards.

Both academic freedom and freedom of speech are basic to the purpose and intellectual integrity of a university. Media, the public and, sometimes, even faculty confuse the two. Presidents, provosts, deans, and department heads should not. Academic freedom is the freedom of faculty to "seek the truth and teach the truth as they see it in their discipline of training" without fear of employment reprisal. Academic tenure, lifetime or term, usually granted after some probationary period, is the reprisal protection mechanism.

Freedom of speech is granted all citizens by the first amendment to the U.S. constitution. However, unless constrained by law or directed by a jurisdictional body in a specific case, freedom of speech, per se, provides no protection from employment reprisal. (See also Chapter 47.)

More than once during your years in the president's job (or that of a provost or dean) you will likely need to make clear, and help committees or others keep clear, that differentiation. And you may need to defend and support a faculty member whose employment status is challenged by the public—or by faculty colleagues or even your governing board—for "seeking or teaching the truth as he or she sees it in his or her discipline of training."

To fully respect and protect academic freedom and tenure also requires that their use is limited to that. Should there be an attempt by a faculty member, committee, or other group to use them for some other purpose, such as to prevent employment reprisal for nonproductivity, violation of university policy, incompetence, or inappropriate activities outside the discipline of training, public respect for academic freedom and tenure is diminished.

Nor should tenure be applied to positions not closely involved in academic research, campus instruction, or extension education. At Kansas State, for example, I encountered a long-standing system of "administrative tenure," granted after years of satisfactory service in several nonacademic units. It was counter to board policy and, because its presence could weaken our ability to defend academic tenure, we gradually abandoned the system.

How about other efforts to constrain research or education, on campus or off? As a young faculty member, I watched leaders of a breed organization march into my department head's office to demand that an extension colleague make no more statements on the small size and enterprise inefficiency of the Southdown breed of sheep. But, my colleague had the data; he was fully supported by the department head.

As a dean, vice-chancellor, or president, I have been challenged by legislators and industry leaders regarding professors' statements on nuclear energy, the economics of ethanol, interest calculation methods used by financial institutions, and the economics of planned irrigation projects. Chapter 23 cites concerns by cattle feeders about feedlot run-off research. Sometimes subtle, sometimes strong and vocal, challenges and reservations are expressed.

As president, you should periodically ask a dean, and a dean should ask a department head, "Is there any industry pressure on your college (or department) to avoid research or instruction, on campus or off, on any sector where such is needed for the long-term benefit of society *or of your clientele?*

I recognize the reality of an industry's political influence and the fragility of state appropriations to the university. I also recognize industry concerns when research discloses new consumer preferences, or demand for a new process or product, that costs the industry time and money to implement—to change production systems or equipment! For example, new environmental regulations based on university research may require considerable expenditure by a manufacturing industry or an individual business. However, if the university fails to figure out how to bring about that needed research or instruction, and if it seems that society or the *long-term interests* of the industries that college or department serves may suffer as a result, the university is not fulfilling what academic freedom and tenure exist to help insure!

How about freedom of speech—and the freedom of a speaker to be heard? This is a different issue from academic freedom, but it should also be a hallmark of your university. More than one university-invited speaker has been dis-invited or their speech heckled to the extent that no one could hear. This has happened to spouses of U.S. presidents, top officials of foreign governments, and people at both ends of the political spectrum. Such events are embarrassing not only to the institution, but to the very concept of higher education.

We once had to clear Kansas State's McCain auditorium, when its sound system at full volume could not drown out the jeering howl of a dozen who had come from elsewhere to protest our speaker, Saudi Oil Minister Sheikh Ahmed Zaki Yamani.[25] Students, staff, and invited guests were then readmitted by identification. The clearing and readmission took more than an hour but the speaker was heard! TV monitors were even provided in the student union for those not readmitted.

On another occasion, when a couple of on-campus groups were disturbed that former President Ian Smith of apartheid Rhodesia (now Zimbabwe) had been invited to speak, we devoted two evenings in our living room negotiating with faculty and student leaders such details as who would join Smith on stage, who would introduce, with whom he would dine, and where. That negotiation let Smith's speech occur without interruption.

From time to time, I received phone calls or letters objecting to a speaker or a movie scheduled for our student union. My response was always, "The responsibility for speakers and movies in the student union lies with the union governing board (students and a few staff) and I think it is best to let them handle any concerns." Though a few letters to the editor appeared and union board members may have gotten some phone calls, I do not recall any follow-up protests to my office.

Your university needs, and most likely has, written institution policies and guidelines that outline who or what groups—student, faculty, or other—are authorized to invite speakers and any conditions that should apply, such as time, location, or notification of campus security. Those not interested in a speaker's message need not attend. Those who want to express opposition can do so in later discussion, in campus media, or by other means that do not interfere with listeners.

Academic freedom, freedom to speak, and freedom to be heard are hallmarks of a strong university.

CHAPTER 39

Faculty and Staff Unions

It seems strange to some that faculty unions are rather common in public universities, but virtually nonexistent in private universities. Would not the potential effect of unions on "participatory management" by faculty be the same in public as in private universities? Why this difference in the presence of faculty unions?

In the case of private universities, according to Saltzman,[26] the U.S. Supreme Court ruled in 1980 in the Yeshiva case (a private university) that professors were bosses, not workers, because they participate in decisions about academic affairs and personnel. As bosses, they are not "employees" under the National Labor Relations Act and therefore do not have a protected right to organize and bargain. State universities, however, function under state law. In many states, laws *require* that public employers bargain with unions having "majority support." In some other states, laws *grant* bargaining rights to certain types of institutions or some categories of employees.

If your university is in a state where law *prohibits* collective bargaining by state employees, you can skip this chapter. At this writing there are four such states: Texas, Alabama, North Carolina, and Virginia. Where unions do exist, a campus may have more than one bargaining unit. It is well to read the negotiated union contract (or contracts) and have any unclear features explained and recent negotiations described.

Here are some things you and other involved members of your management team should look for:

1. Is the bargaining unit contract with the university or with the governing board? In the case of a multi-university system, is the contract system-wide or with the individual university?

2. How is the (each, if several) bargaining unit defined? Is there one unit and contract for faculty and one for classified staff? Is the faculty unit university-wide, or are certain colleges excluded or in separate units? How about nonfaculty professional staff? How about graduate students?
3. For a faculty union, what are the constraints, requirements, or provisions regarding participation in faculty senate or university councils and committees?
4. Is the union affiliated with a state or national organization, such as the American Association of University Professors, National Education Association or American Federation of Teachers? (Some other unions, such as the Service Employees International Union, have focused on organizing graduate assistants.)
5. Who does the negotiating for the University (or system) and who does it for the bargaining unit?
6. Between contract negotiations the primary union focus is on resolving grievances. What procedures are established for their resolution?

A university with a faculty union is fortunate if a contract permits retaining a functional administrative structure, yet insures appropriate faculty participation in academic matters. For example: Are department heads part of the bargaining unit? How about deans? How about professors who are also institute or center directors? How about part-time faculty?

It is well to note whether contract provisions provide any constraints on faculty participation in search-and-screening or tenure and promotion committees, or in curriculum and other issues where faculty input is vital.

Both the literature and those who have worked with faculty unions indicate that when problems develop, they usually result from (1) failure of university administrators or unit leaders to follow terms of a contract or (2) legislative appropriation provisions, new state laws, or court rulings that may be considered in conflict with contract terms. Unions generally favor across-the-board pay increases, but legislators, governing boards and administrations usually lean toward merit. It is not uncommon for appropriation bills to carry a provision that X dollars or Y percent of funds shall be used for such as "merit increases," "teachers of undergraduates," or "the most productive ten percent" of the faculty. Should the bargaining unit play a role in developing the criteria for distributing such salary increase money? Or, should those specific funds be considered outside the terms of the contract?

A state university faculty union example: In the South Dakota system, there is an encompassing contract between the system's board of regents and a "Council on Higher Education," an affiliate of the state unit of the National Education Association. SDSU Provost Carol Peterson indicates that campus administrative attention is therefore largely focused on seeing to it that deans and department heads, especially those newly appointed, are familiar with contract terms and that the terms are followed in developing or revising performance standards in teaching, research or extension, and in faculty evaluations.

Should you and your university face faculty union issues, the series of court rulings described by Saltzman may be instructive. In the case of bargaining units and contracts for nonfaculty, basic issues apply and principles hold. Little is unique.

PART VI

Focus on Funding

Richard Rominger of Winters, California, a relatively new regent for the 10-campus University of California, recently told me, "Reduction in proportion of state funding is changing state universities to 'state-assisted' universities. In the past four years, University of California enrollment increased 19 percent and state support decreased 15 percent." Former University of Missouri Board Member Turner says it differently, "State legislatures are making a huge mistake; they are privatizing state universities. They are making them dependent, in both programs and facilities, on who gives the most money!"

Whereas 80 percent or more of most state university budgets came from state appropriated funds in the first half of the twentieth century, it is now well below 40 percent in most and below ten percent in some. A 2005 study of four-year college presidents indicated that budget and financial issues "permeate almost every facet of the top job" on campuses.[10] You and certain members of your management team will divide your fund-seeking effort among four major sources: state appropriations, student and other fees, government grants and contracts, and private funds, the latter including individual donors as well as corporations and organizations. Each is discussed in the chapters that follow.

The average state university gets about a quarter of its total expenditure money from each of the four sources. For major research universities the percentage from government grants and contracts is much higher. For some others, the percentage from student fees is higher.

This is not just a matter for you and your central management team and foundation; the need for funds impacts the behavior and time allocation of virtually every university unit and many faculty and staff. Research, extension, and some teaching faculty seek grants for their projects, to finance not only supplies, technicians, and graduate assistants, but often their own salaries or portions thereof. Deans and department heads work with foundation staff to seek scholarship, program, or construction funds from interested donors. Student tuition and fees have escalated rapidly and campus, area, or county extension staff impose or increase fees for conferences, short courses, and even 4-H membership and activities.

The chapters in this section speak to both these trends in funding and how you and your management team can deal with the realities and consequences of these trends.

CHAPTER

State Appropriations

I n 1985, 17 percent of the Virginia's general fund budget went to its state colleges and universities; in 2004 the figure was 10 percent.[27] That trend is illustrative of most states and is a consequence of competition for state funds by corrections, social programs, primary and secondary education, and other worthy needs. Yet, state university costs for salaries, fringe benefits, equipment, supplies, and travel have escalated rapidly, enrollment has increased, and society expects more university involvement in the states' economic and social growth. Further, state policies and regulations may inhibit their state universities from adapting to such realities in a business-like way.

Virginia's university and political leaders addressed this latter issue "head-on." A recent "Restructured Higher Education Financial and Administrative Operations Act" would grant university authority for certain financial and administrative operations in return for certain commitments to the state.[27] Under a "management agreement" that would be approved by the governor and general assembly, university governing boards would carry full responsibility for capital outlay, procurement, information technology, human resources (including salaries at market level), and setting tuition and fees. The agreement would include a multi-year university operating plan (financial, academic, and enrollment data) and a guarantee that tuition would not be a barrier to access (through increased financial aid and agreements with the community college system).

States vary, of course, in their imposed regulations and authorities over state university operation. To the extent that law allows, governing boards in most states have moved their university leadership at least *toward* the entrepreneurial features of this Virginia plan.

No matter the proportion of the state budget going to higher education, or the decrease in proportion, the university is yet a state resource and the dollars are significant! Getting what you can for your university and for higher education is still a top priority, one of your major tasks. Regardless of the state's higher education structure or the details of the appropriation and money-allocation process, you will have important dealings with the governor and the legislature. They need to be profitable dealings.

It was early December, my first year as president. After a speech to our local Rotary Club, Kansas Governor Bob Bennett, a man with seemingly perfect memory, asked me, "Why did you reverse the top two buildings from last year's Kansas State capital improvement priorities?" (We were seeking architectural planning money, the first step for construction.)

"I didn't, that was done by the Regents' staff!" Our six-university system board staff had presented all capital improvement requests at a separate budget hearing with the governor a few days before. I had learned later that, at the last minute and without consulting me, the staff had reversed our top-priority, a classroom-office building (later named Bluemont Hall), and our second-ranked agronomy building. To put it mildly, I had been disappointed in the staff. The shift would cause me problems with our Education and Psychology faculty who were scheduled to occupy Bluemont.

Beyond that, the move *ignored the strength* of statewide political support for that agronomy building. A dozen or more farm organizations, from the corn growers to conservation districts had passed resolutions of support and were periodically reminding legislators and the governor of the need. *By the agronomy building remaining Number 2, its political support could get us both!*

Some school superintendents might have been aware that our education faculty needed new offices, but they and the state school board association's political efforts were focused on money for public schools. If Bluemont remained in the Number 2 spot we would likely work and wait for years to get it funded. I was glad for the governor's question, and he followed up, "What is your priority?"

"Classroom-Office (Bluemont) Number 1; Agronomy Number 2!"

The governor went on to express doubt there would be money in his budget for *any* architectural planning. Tax revenues did not look good and "Besides, even if the universities would get money for architects, they would likely change their design or the planned site before there would be money for construction."

"Governor," I said, "If we get the architectural planning money, I guarantee any building will be built as designed and where it is now planned!" I did not like the planned location for Bluemont (and I still do not), but the site had been chosen before my time and, I had learned, only after intense debate. With growing enrollment we sorely needed the space.

Come January, planning money for *both* buildings was in the governor's recommendation to the legislature, with the classroom-office building (Bluemont) Number 1 and agronomy (later named Throckmorton Hall) Number 2. The legislature concurred, and construction money came a year later.

Four things are usually needed for state appropriations: (1) a clear message of need and how funds would be used, (2) board approval, (3) inclusion in the governor's budget recommendation—or willingness to accept if the legislature adds the item, and (4) understanding and support by key legislators.

Before my first presentation to the joint appropriations committee of the South Dakota legislature as an SDSU dean, I received some good advice from Dr. Herndon Honstead, a Kansas State graduate who was USDA area veterinarian located in Pierre and a careful observer of legislative behavior. "Tell them the dollars you need, what you will spend it for, and why. If they give you the money, spend it for *that!* Also, tell them the dollars you will need for the next step. And when next year comes, follow through with that dollar request." Governors and legislators have good memories and they do not want to feel misled. Tell them the straight story; they will remember!

Except where a program or building is part of his or her political agenda, a governor rarely has time to personally view capital or program needs of the state's many institutions and agencies. Governors may make ceremonial campus visits but they largely depend on governing boards and their staff to prioritize university needs. Legislators, however, especially members of appropriations or capital improvement committees, often want to see and hear.

There was no statewide chemistry lobby to build political support for a new chemistry building we needed at Kansas State; we had to sell the need on safety and overcrowding. Over a three-year period, my biochemistry and chemistry department heads, my legislative assistant, and I led at least a dozen legislator groups through the acid fumes of student-packed laboratories and around the rusted-out exhaust vents in the attic of our 1930's Willard Hall. Sometimes the spouses would come along to the campus for a coffee at our home, but my wife would get them through the chemistry building while legislators were looking at some other project.

Opportunities abound—industry conferences on campus, recognition events, and, especially, football and basketball games—to get legislators onto the campus or to out-state units. They not only can see needs, they also want to see how *their previous appropriations* were used.

Every political process carries some risk. Our board had approved our seeking a separate "line item" operating budget for our college of veterinary medicine. Because university appropriations were based in part on a system-wide student credit formula, we had been shortchanging other disciplines to provide the ratio of faculty to students needed for good veterinary education.

Unfortunately, we failed to convince either Governor Bennett or the Senate president, a Kansas State graduate, on the idea of a separate line-item for Veterinary Medicine. However, my legislative assistant, Dr. Barry Flinchbaugh, had established a very close relationship with the chair of the senate appropriations committee, about equal in political power to the senate president, and to the appropriations chair the idea made sense. If we could get the separate budget through the legislature, we expected no problem in getting the governor's approval. But the Senate president was another matter. Should we press ahead?

We did. With the senate appropriations committee chair leading the effort, the separate budget not only cleared both the senate and house, it was sharply enhanced with some additional positions, and Governor Bennett signed the bill. With Veterinary Medicine now removed from the student credit formula system, we would have more teaching positions for the rest of the university. A big win!

But a residual problem remained. The Senate appropriations chair did not seek re-election and the Senate president remained. And, there happened to be another Kansas State issue—a coal-fired power plant—that had distressed the senate president. Flinchbaugh, whom I had brought in from an extension public policy position in the economics department because of his extraordinary ability to convince—and he had done that well with the key legislators—had to go back to his public policy position (where he became a popular government adviser on national policy).

One should not overlook the opportunities that legislative problems and "special investigations" present. They may begin as a legislative concern and end with more money or a new building for the university. The burned-out shell of Nichols Gym, a remnant of student unrest days and dubbed "the Castle" by generations of students, awaited me when I became president and I pledged to both the students and myself that I would "resolve the problem." Conservationists wanted it rebuilt, but the dimensions and location just did not fit high priority facility needs and several years elapsed.

In the middle of a legislative session, a bill emerged in the state senate to appropriate $250,000 to "either raze the building and clear the site or stabilize it as a permanent ruin." Key legislators wanted to help me solve the problem; the appropriations committee chair asked me to choose the option and the legislature would proceed to appropriate the money.

Choosing the option would be contentious; if ever, that was a time for a broad campus committee. I called together all key administrators and faculty and student leaders. There was strong debate, but eventually a majority said "Tear it down and clear the site." That seemed the practical solution, but I knew the conservationists' emotions were intense. That evening I walked around the shell several times, still considering options. I did the same the next morning, then called those on campus I could reach and told them that my recommendation to the appropriations committee would be: "stabilize and preserve the entrance—the heavy wooden doors, the surrounding arch stone-work, and the ramp, up which student cavalry caissons had entered in the building's early days—and raze the balance." Their responses were consistently supportive, and I called the committee chair.

His response, "Good plan. Consider it done." I relaxed, but not for long. By noon committee action was on the air, word spread across campus, and some students began organizing a caravan to Topeka and the legislature to "Save the Castle." Those students spent the next day in Topeka, buttonholed legislators, and I received a call late in the day from my local state representative, John Stites, asking me to withdraw my recommendation. Neither he *nor most of his colleagues* could resist the student pressure, but he did not want to vote against his home university president. I told him I needed to think about it.

We had another "committee meeting" the next morning, the group concurred in my withdrawing, and I made the call. But, I added to Stites. "Now, it is your problem." The outcome? An ad hoc house-senate committee was named to study the issue and bring a recommendation to the following year's legislature. Three years later, my wife and I were driven up to the heavy wooden doors of the "Castle" in a horse-drawn carriage to greet, in tux and gown, our Foundation Presidents' Club members for their spring gala in the open halls and foyer of a fully reconstructed building (at higher cost than new construction would have been). It housed both our computer science and speech departments, including a theatre in the round, where Club members watched a student performance of Harry Truman's life. Though the evening was meant as a celebration—generous donors joining in welcoming back to full function a historic structure—I could not miss a parallel as I watched the performance—the heat that Truman took and the heat a university president takes for making necessary decisions and seeing that problems get resolved.

As citizens we may joke that "no one is safe while the legislature is in session" and a state legislature may sometimes be a challenge or a frustration. However, with rare exception, I have found state legislators to be serious, thoughtful, and constructive, wanting very much to do the right thing. Each legislator will have some biases, priorities, loyalties, and concerns. It is up to you, as university president, or key staff, to find out what those are and to see that your university's case is presented in ways that allow the legislators—and the governor—to support your university's board-approved needs. Though not as generous as we would like, state appropriations are rather dependable and, in most cases, a highly significant part of a university's budget base.

I consider the second part of the budget base to be fees: student fees and a good many others, the subject of Chapter 41.

CHAPTER 41

Student and Other Fees

I spent a recent evening seeking resident undergraduate tuition and fee information via eight state university websites. This is what I found:

1. Only on two sites did I rather quickly find a student fee schedule. In both cases, they were detailed and precise, by college and by service (instruction, recreation, health, season tickets, etc.).
2. In the other six cases, tuition and fees were not easily found. Regardless of the term I chose to click, the "Financial Aids and Scholarship" or "Financing Your Education" page appeared.
3. On five of those university sites I *eventually* found tuition and fee schedules. They ranged, in content, from detailed and precise to an estimate and a reference to additional fees in certain named colleges.
4. On the sixth site, after clicking every likely topic, I found a fee table well down on the "Frequently Asked Questions" page.
5. Only one of the universities showed a single university-wide tuition/fee charge for all, regardless of college.
6. Differential tuition or additional college, technology, or equipment fees were shown in one or more cases for engineering, architecture, medicine, law, pharmacy, home economics, education, agriculture, and veterinary medicine. One university had a per-credit technology fee for every college, in addition to the university-wide per-credit tuition.

Differential tuition rates among colleges are logical; many professional colleges, especially medicine and veterinary medicine, provide a high teacher–student ratio and require costly equipment and supplies. However, the additional college fees shown on some of those websites appeared to have little relationship to relative instructional costs. Some colleges whose courses are mostly lecture and discussion had a higher technology fee than others that require extensively-equipped laboratories and a high teacher–student ratio. This caused me to question, "Were some of those fees imposed because the market would bear it, or had administrative allocation of appropriated funds to individual colleges not kept pace with enrollment or technology costs and, therefore, fees had been added to make up the difference?"

It is well for you to review the fee structure in your university and the rationale for fee differentials or "add-ons?" Do they reflect real cost? Demand? Future income of graduates?

It is clear that in most of the university websites I studied, the focus in prospective student communication is not on fees per se, but rather on net cost, the *difference* between financial aid (scholarships, grants, loans, and work study) and the fees. Such has also been expressed as a worthy principle by trustees with whom I have visited. And, it is that net cost that comes through in my visits with university-bound students and their parents.

The feedback I get from students, parents, finance officers, and trustees also tells me that the fee structure in many state universities is due some more changes. The rare university-wide, per-semester tuition charge for "12 credits or more," for example, will not long survive. Beyond that, with the realities of limited state funding, differential instructional costs, student mobility, more part-time and commuting students, and heavy recruitment by competing universities, you and key members of your management team will talk "fee for service," "pricing policy." and "market drivers." Discussions will be based on cost analyses and demographic and other data. As budget pressure and more sophisticated data-based management are implemented, I suggest most state universities will have most of the following (some have most now):

1. An application/admission fee for application materials, application review, and the cost of setting up records.
2. A per-credit tuition rate, likely differentiated among disciplines and perhaps among course levels.
3. A partial or zero refund from dropping a course and a service charge for other course changes.
4. An academic advising fee for regularly scheduled visits with a designated adviser in the students' major plus aptitude/interest tests or profiles.
5. A "season ticket" fee for all or certain university sports or cultural events.
6. Membership fee for use of recreation facilities.
7. For those without other coverage, a health insurance fee (premium).
8. Some periodically announced "special deals," for students to fill a low-enrollment course or to attract students into a new curriculum.

With known costs of providing each item, per-student or per-credit, management can make a judgment regarding how much of that cost, above the specific fee income, should be subsidized by other university funds. Such cost analyses and subsidizing judgments have been made for some time in other university services, such as medical and veterinary clinics, diagnostic laboratories, speech and psychological testing, or water and soil analyses.

Clinics and diagnostic laboratories on state university campuses have generally been subsidized in order to help insure that people will bring suspected human-risk or animal-risk cases to the laboratories for rapid and accurate diagnoses or to clinics for treatment. When a new risk emerges, such as a highly contagious human or animal disease, new state or federal funds may also come and help subsidize the service cost. For less critical services, state budget pressures, industry advances, and interests of private sector providers have prompted significant fee increases or the dropping of some services.

4-H and other youth programs (mostly led by the state land grant universities), with both limited funds and enrollment growth, have, in many states, imposed fees for membership and for related activities. Such fees have not dampened enrollment; membership continues to grow. Fortunately, in most states and counties, private funds have been raised to insure that no youth is denied membership or active participation for lack of money.

People respect more highly what they pay for. Manufacturing clientele who pay a fee for process or product consultation will listen, ask questions, discuss options, and likely test out the advice thoroughly. Those who pay a registration fee for an extension workshop will more likely arrive on time, pay careful attention to what is presented, read handout materials, and implement more of what they learned. Students who buy a separate season ticket may attend more sports and cultural events.

It is with some reticence that I suggest a separate fee for academic advising. I have long considered academic advising as important as quality instruction and, for some, perhaps more important. High-ability students can be aggressively challenged by an effective adviser and encouraged to reach for greater heights, both in course work and career aspirations. Lesser-ability students' can be guided in course selection or the pace (course credits per term) that is in accordance with their skills, allowing them to leave the university with a positive experience, whether it is with or without a degree.

In some state universities and colleges, academic advising appears to be an "afterthought," an "overload," or at least inconsistent in quality. If a separate fee were charged for full academic advising services—an assigned faculty member in the major (or college, if no major has been chosen), well trained for the function, basing their advice in part on ACT/SAT scores and high school transcripts, time budgeted for advising, and with back-up professional testing or profiling services—I believe most students and parents would happily pay the fee. They would also, then, expect high quality advising service and the university would more certainly provide it.

Such a list of separate fees may preclude student-initiated fees for construction, renovation, or additions to basketball arenas or such (unless such are built into a season ticket fee). Such would also lead to—and perhaps has in some universities—university residence hall or apartment lease arrangements with or without membership in the university recreation facility, and/or other combinations.

Student loans. Any discussion of student fees cannot be complete without mention of student loans. Keeping those federal funds and guarantees coming for student loan programs is critical to enrollment. But to many graduates, the resultant cumulative debt is a "ball and chain." Cumulative debt of $50,000 is not uncommon for a B.A. or B.S. graduate and perhaps $100,000 for an M.D. or Ph.D. Bank officers have shared with me too many cases of young couples or individuals with so much college debt that handling mortgage payments on the house they want, or interest on operating credit they would need to start a new business, is out of the question. Though with solid degrees, they already have all the debt they can handle—or more—and are destined to salaried jobs, a modest rental home or, in some cases, default on debt!

Former Wisconsin Regent Chair Tom Lyon speaks clearly to this in a higher education system self-critique, "We justify higher tuition by increasing student loan levels, an economically flawed practice." And, he adds another concern, "At our major public universities, middle and lower income families are becoming severely underrepresented." He cited the Madison campus, where "the average family income of its undergraduates is approaching $100,000."

Student loans, grants, and "work study" funds determine, in an increasing number of cases, where a student will enroll and, perhaps, whether they can enroll. You, your management team, and members of your governing board face both a management issue and a social policy issue in student fees.

CHAPTER

Grants, Contracts and Earmarks

Two major factors caused a Bob Dole Communications Building to be built on the Kansas State campus: (1) After several of our board members flew with me to see such a facility at Oklahoma State University, and the value of the program it housed, the board supported moving this building to the top of our capital improvement request list. (2) U.S. Senate Majority Leader (and Kansas' senior senator) Dole and his staff identified federal programs through which $5.9 million of federal funds were eventually provided. Certainly there were other factors, but those were the keys.

After our board had endorsed the project, Mike Johnson, my legislative assistant, and I spent most of a day with one of Senator Dole's staff, studying the budget categories of several federal departments. With the senator's seniority and leadership post, the issue was not whether federal funds could be earmarked; it was which federal agency budgets would be the most logical vehicles.

According to Citizens Against Government Waste (CAGW), the F05 federal budget had 13,997 earmarks[28]. Since FY '95, the federal dollars in earmarks had nearly tripled, but the *number* of earmarks in FY '05 was *more than ten times* the number in FY '95. The practice of earmarking by members of Congress has *extended far beyond* such multi-million dollar items as military systems or major federal buildings. A few minutes on the CAGW website will reveal a good many earmarks in the $200,000 to million dollar category, many to universities.

In the first budget I handled as assistant secretary for science and education in USDA, I had three pages of such line items to administer through my four agencies. Most I considered worthy—research and education endeavors near the top of any list our staff, industry leadership, or university faculty in human nutrition, biotechnology, veterinary medicine, or agriculture would recommend. A few, however, would be of little value in advancing the U.S. food system or U.S. agriculture. Some were hardly related.

Some earmarks do not show up in appropriations bills. They are only in appropriations committee reports, the written guidance not formally approved by Congressional vote nor carrying the president's signature. In such a report, there may be a statement, such as, "It is the intent of the committee that of the amount appropriated for X agency, Y amount shall be used to establish and operate a nuclear engineering research institute on the central Great Plains." Though the university is not named, Kansas State would fit that description. And, if that agency wanted favorable treatment in its next budget, considering the committee membership, it would see to it that Kansas State submitted a proposal for funding and that the proposal was funded.

I serve on an advisory committee to a multi-million dollar agricultural marketing project involving the University of California, Iowa State University, and Kansas State University, with some subcontracting to Oklahoma State, and funded, not through USDA's Science and Education budget, but through its Rural Development budget. The *parent multi-year authorization* bill provides that the project will receive "five percent of that amount appropriated *each year* to Value-Added Development Grants." Though this is an unusual form of earmark, it supports the logic that research should disclose and education should convey knowledge and information in accordance with the volume of such processing businesses under development. At the same time, it certainly helps insure stability and continuity to staffing and operations in four state universities! It is also evident that more than one state's senators and House members likely played a role in the wording of that authorization bill!

There may also be state earmarks. When it became clear in the early 2000s that about $400 million from the tobacco industry would come to the state of Michigan (the result of group legal action by a number of state attorneys-general), Michigan State President Peter McPherson enlisted President Lee Bollinger of the University of Michigan to join with him in proposing that the tobacco money to be received by the state finance a major step forward in life sciences research. Specifically, they proposed and their governor drove formation of a Michigan Life Sciences Corridor (now called the Technology Tri-Corridor). The tobacco money provided up to $50 million per year for competitive-bid research and technology commercialization.

Coincident with the writing of this work, I have made two trips to Washington. The first was to accompany a university project leader to exploratory meetings with program funding units in the U.S. Agency for International Development, USDA, and a private consortium that had federal funds for subcontracting. On the second trip, largely for visits with higher education associations and former university presidents, I was in several office buildings near the Capitol. In one of those buildings were offices of six universities, one Ivy-league, one private and predominantly black, and four state universities.

I visited with several staff in those offices and asked how they spend their time. The response: "Mostly with members of Congress and their staff, either seeking earmarks or, in concert with other universities' Washington staff, seeking higher appropriation levels in the education (including those student loan, Pell grant, and loan guarantee programs) or research and development budgets of federal agencies." "How about help for individual faculty seeking grants and contracts?" I asked. The response: "Most of them already have contacts and know where the funds are. We may help track some of their proposals or, in some cases, suggest to a Congressional staff member they make a phone call of encouragement to the granting agency."

A president and others in university leadership need to be "poised to pounce" in Washington, or in response to Washington. How many new university laboratories were established and funded and how many existing labs had their budgets materially augmented, as the result of 9/11? The public became security minded; Congress responded.

Though I believe most of the U.S. citizenry supports the federal appropriations to student aid, many bemoan the numerous Congressional earmarks. University leadership, however, must recognize the reality; power in university research and other program priorities—money allocation—has shifted *toward* Washington. From where did it shift? With proportionally less money from state legislatures, the allocation authority shifted largely *from* governing boards, university presidents, provosts, deans and department heads!

When most university funds were state appropriated or came to universities by established federal formulas (such as Hatch funds for agricultural research or Smith-Lever funds for cooperative extension), university leadership generally determined research and statewide extension program priorities, with faculty and clientele input and advice. Today the priority setting that can be exercised by a president, provost, dean, or department head is *largely* in the faculty hiring process, in allocating the limited state appropriations and grant overhead funds to *build expertise and capacity that will warrant grant and contract funding,* and in the support given to proposal writing and Washington follow-up.

Now, let me present another perspective, as a user of research/extension output who has worked in both universities and federal agencies, who recognizes the value of a "systems approach" to increasingly costly and complex issues, and who now devotes considerable time to such an issue, U.S. energy security. A federal agency with *both* in-house research capability and grant/contract funds for tapping university *and* industry talent can bring about rapid progress on a national priority. The DOE National Renewable Energy Laboratory (NREL) at Golden, Colorado, is an example. It can plan and implement *a systems approach,* along with other DOE entities, to renewable transportation fuels, from engine design through bio-fuel specifications and refinery processes to the refinery feedstock—and *to each component thereof.*

One component is ligno-cellulosic feedstock (such as native grasses and trees), which, in terms of available volume and net energy gain, has an enormous potential to provide ethanol. It dwarfs corn, now the major U.S. ethanol feedstock. But a bottleneck to economic use of the ligno-cellulosic feedstock has been the lack of enzymes to degrade the diverse and complex ligno-cellulosic molecules. NREL assembled *in-house, university, and industry* scientists to identify promising options and the scientists that could address each option, issued requests for proposals, allocated funds, and coordinated communication among the several research efforts. The consequence: In a four-year period enough bacterial enzymes were identified or developed (mostly by genetic engineering of bacterium lines) to lower the enzyme cost for producing a gallon of ligno-cellulosic ethanol *from six dollars to 20 cents*.

At this writing, ethanol from such feedstock is not yet cost competitive with ethanol from corn or sugar beets (simpler molecules) or with petroleum-based gasoline, but NREL and its cooperating and funded scientists are getting close.

Energy security is only an example. Many of our major economic, technological, and societal problems are as broad and complex—and as costly to solve—as energy security. Each may require many dollars and, for reasonable efficiency and speed of resolution, a "systems approach." Policy leaders consider federal grant and contract programs in that context. That is reality. The task for the university scientist and unit leader is to find the niche—the grant or contract program—within a "problem resolution system" where their skills and facilities can make a useful contribution worthy of funding.

And, although political earmarking is under fire by some key U.S. senators at this writing, it is reality.

CHAPTER 43

Donors and the University Foundation

olding his hat, an elderly gentleman stepped into the Kansas State president's office and told my receptionist that he wanted to talk with someone about making a gift to the university in his will. In my absence, our visitor was led to my assistant who listened. The visitor told her he had never married, had worked in the southeast Kansas coal mines, and had saved some money. Several nieces and nephews had attended Kansas State, had done well, and he wanted to help other young people get Kansas State degrees. He had taken a bus to Manhattan and a taxi to the campus. He wanted to get to the right office, get arrangements made, and be back at the bus station in time to catch the bus back home.

She escorted him to our foundation office where he and a staff member discussed the details. He caught his bus home, foundation staff followed up, and years later his estate executor sent a check for several hundred thousand dollars to the Kansas State University Foundation.

Such stories are not uncommon in the history of state universities. In this century, however, state university foundations are not just recipients of money for scholarships or other university "extras." They are well-staffed, aggressive, fundraising enterprises critical to both university programs and facilities. In early 2005, the University of Iowa Foundation reported 144 full-time employees, Iowa State's reported 78, and University of Northern Iowa's reported 28. At this writing, the top foundation officer may be in the $200,000 or higher annual salary and a number of experienced staff may be in the $100,000 plus category.[29]

Although private colleges have always depended heavily on endowments for operations, it was not until 1944 that one of my Kansas State predecessors, Milton Eisenhower, enlisted three local businessmen to help form an "endowment association" to solicit and handle private funds. In the latter part of the twentieth century, with state funding lagging well behind inflation and university needs, more private funds became essential.

At the same time, with rapid growth in individuals' asset values—common stock, real estate, and other—coupled with tax laws and regulations that encouraged private giving, state universities saw alumni and friends as potential sources of major funds. *Annual* giving to some state university foundations at this writing is in the hundreds of millions.

University foundations *spend* considerable money to raise private money. In FY '04, the Kansas State Foundation spent a bit more than four million dollars for salary, travel, and other fund raising costs and took in more than $42 million in donations.[30] That was a great return on investment! When interest, dividends, and asset gain were added to the donations, total income far exceeded the $42 million. Among university foundations, dollars spent per hundred dollars raised generally range from seven or eight to as high as 18.[31]

What are your roles as university president (deans and department heads also play most of the roles)?

1. Cultivate donors and ask for money. It is part of your job. You set the pattern and also the expectation for others of your team. People admire universities and their leadership. Any association with the president, a dean, or department head adds purpose and dignity to their lives. Their interest and support can be cultivated; they will respond well.

2. You should have a close working relationship with the foundation board and management. So should your vice president for finance. The foundation executive officer needs complete communication with university leadership on program and construction priorities and plans. So, too, does the foundation board. There needs to be a formal agreement between the university and foundation, spelling out relationships and prerogatives. Fortunately, the two national associations, the Association of Governing Boards of Universities and Colleges and the Council for Advancement and Support of Education, have jointly developed a set of guidelines for such.[32]

3. Involve donors and potential donors in university plans and projects. The University of Iowa had $14 million of state money for a new engineering building in the early 1990s but needed well over six million more. An alumnus who had been asked to serve on the building steering committee urged the university foundation board to make the private fund target big enough to do the total job. He and his company followed up with sizeable donations (and so did others), and the building was completed as planned

4. Coordinate policy with the foundation and the university governing board on the naming of buildings, conference rooms, gardens, or others for major donors. Some university/foundation policies are specific, with naming rights based on number of dollars or proportion of total cost; the same for endowed and named professorships. Should honorary degrees be used for recognizing donors? If so, should not criteria be established?

5. See that expenditure procedures and approvals for university projects from dedicated foundation accounts parallel those for university funds. This is discussed more fully in Chapter 8.

How about major capital campaigns? As this chapter was being drafted, the University of Arkansas successfully completed a seven-year, billion-dollar campaign. At least 25 universities, including 15 state universities, recently had capital campaigns of that size or a larger goal. UCLA just completed a $2.5 billion campaign.

Arkansas' Associate Vice Chancellors for Development, Sandra and Clay Edwards, emphasize that for such campaign success, the fund-raising objectives must be linked directly to the "action side of the University mission—the strategic objectives of the university and the individual colleges." Potential donors are, in some respects, like appropriations committees of legislatures. If the university and its colleges know and clearly state where they want to go, donors "will help the university get there." They will contribute more readily and in larger amounts, especially if the list of university goals and needs includes specific programs or projects that fit the donors' interests. For example, Tyson Foods, the world's largest meat processor, through its own foundation, gave the $12.5 million that put the Arkansas campaign over the top, designating the money largely to programs of their interest in the colleges of business and agriculture.

Recruiting the right people for campaign leadership is critical and you, as president, should play a major role in that recruitment process. If the campaign has the right people in the leadership structure, as well as the right message and top quality foundation staff, those leaders see to it that the campaign is successful. John Tyson, chairman and CEO of Tyson Foods, was vice chairman of the Arkansas campaign.

Should you become president in the middle of a campaign, your role will likely be with certain potential donors not previously willing to make a major commitment. If their reticence relates to some problem with the university, your new face and perspective may just be what lets them come on board.

Deans and certain department heads are important actors in a capital campaign. Each may have specific program and dollar campaign targets, a segment of the total program goal. Each can speak most authoritatively about the need and the opportunity in their sector. And, each should have developed good rapport with potential donors, including individuals, associations, corporations, and foundations.

Should an outside consulting firm be used in planning or conducting a major campaign? It depends on the university's history in fund-raising and the depth of foundation staff experience. If such is limited, consultants can be especially helpful. They can lay the groundwork with potential campaign leaders and donors, ferret out their interests and their giving potential. They can also absorb any complaints about some university program or staff member. They can emphasize the long-term university benefit, benefit that transcends the complaint target.

What other private fund-raising issues might you face as a new president?

1. Are there other fund-raising units in or related to the university? If so—and there usually are—you need to insure coordination. There may be a 4-H Foundation, an Athletic Foundation or Boosters Club, and a museum or art center with its own fund-raising staff and dollar target. Both the university and donors risk embarrassment if coordination of either policy or contact is absent.

2. A high proportion of foundation receipts is dedicated to specific purposes—a named scholarship, a building project, or a department, or an individual staff member's program. You and foundation staff need to insure that the terms of each gift are adhered to. More than one university has been embarrassed—and retention of assets challenged—by failure to follow the terms of a gift.

3. Are donations to the foundation public information? Some donors prefer to remain anonymous or want the donation amount held confidential. To avoid the public disclosure requirements of state laws, most university foundations have established themselves as private entities, located in nonuniversity facilities, and severed other formal connections, such as joint employees. However, even with such arrangements, some courts have held that the public has a right to know the details of virtually any foundation activity related to the state university.

4. You, and perhaps others of your staff, may receive supplemental salary, travel, and entertainment funds, or have funded insurance or retirement programs through the foundation. Should that information be public? You are a state employee, hired by and reporting to the governing board. I believe that all features of employment, including any funds provided through the foundation, should be approved by the University governing board and be available to the public. As a public figure and as a model for other staff, you should consider no less.

5. Where a gift brings with it an annual operating budget requirement, as would be true for a new museum or art center, I suggest that you and foundation staff attempt to see to it that a portion of the gift—or an accompanying gift—is placed in an endowment account to provide operating and maintenance funds. It is tempting for a major donor to suggest, "If I give $10 million for this wonderful facility, certainly the president can find enough money to operate it." Reality is that you probably cannot, without robbing the instruction or some other program budget. An established foundation policy can be a big help in early discussions with donors.

The *constant* for you and your total management team is cultivation of donors and potential donors—knowing them, demonstrating interest in them and their families, visiting their offices when in the vicinity, seeking advice, appointing them to advisory committees or the foundation board, and entertaining them. You should remind yourself that, though some may decline board or "major donor club" membership, avoid public recognition, and want to be anonymous in their contribution, virtually everyone enjoys being "cultivated." And, for some, the ultimate in cultivation is to propose that he or she be a lead donor for a major project. Further, in that cultivation, you should consider that the spouse just may be the major decision-maker and donor.

The president's home, especially if on campus, is a major cultivation asset. How meaningful an invitation to the president's home is may not be so evident to those of us who have lived there. But, it is is! Every significant donor to the major capital campaign of my presidency had been in our home—for a dinner, an evening with some visiting dignitary, such as Red Skelton, or even a reception for a commencement party. A backyard barbecue for our foundation Presidents' Club donors on a football Saturday became a popular fall event. In the winter or spring, we had catered dinners for those major donors in such locations as the university library (which needed renovation funds), the lobby of a new engineering building, and, as mentioned in Chapter 40, the foyer and balcony of the rebuilt "castle."

Two more points: (1) Some of the largest donors to state universities are not alumni of those universities; some have never gone to college, or started college and dropped out. Donors give money, including large sums, for a variety of reasons. Some who were denied, or who by-passed, the university experience, may hold your university in such a high regard that they see a major donation as their way of "associating" with the university. (2) Put in your own money. Join your foundation's Presidents Club. When you demonstrate personal dedication to the private giving effort, deans, department heads, and faculty will follow. And, it surely sends a positive message to external donors.

PART VII

Tending Relationships

As the new president of a state university, you will deal with many constituent groups, often with conflicting demands. Both the number of groups and the conflicting demands can be frustrating. The degree of your frustration or, conversely, your degree of comfort, is likely dependent, I suggest, on two things:

1. Experience in dealing with constituents. If you come by way of the faculty–department head–dean–provost route, where virtually all responsibility has been on campus, you can feel both overwhelmed and uncomfortable. You will encounter concerns of an alumni board, emotions of athletics boosters, penetrating questions of governing board members, or perhaps "university attack" machinations of some legislator or columnist. If you come to a presidency with experience as a director of public affairs, dean of a college with collaborative industry programs, leader of a government agency, or a private business unit, or having defended a budget before a legislative committee, you will be less intimidated and more comfortable.

2. Having a full perspective of each of the constituent groups. See to it that you know their purpose, how they look at the world, their major interests in the university, and their potential value to the university's operations and its future. You should consider each constituency group an asset to the university, with potential to become an even more valuable asset.

The following chapters detail some principles and illustrations that may help you minimize the frustration and maximize the comfort and satisfaction of working with them.

CHAPTER 44

The Governing Board

When I expressed envy to a presidential friend who had his own governing board, he countered, "But, with six universities your board does not have time to meddle in your management!" He was correct on that score. In my 11 years as president, only twice did a board member visibly second-guess a management or personnel action. Members may have thought some of my actions ill-advised, but even those that evoked campus debate or off-campus complaint were consistently and solidly supported.

In 2002, remarks to the NASULGC, The Ohio State University Board Chair Jim Patterson listed the roles of his board:[33]

1. Ensure proper direction for the institution—mission, vision, strategic priorities, plans, and policies.
2. Ensure fiduciary accountability, both financial and legal.
3. Ensure maintenance of key relationships with external constituencies.
4. Ensure effective governance of affiliated entities.
5. Ensure superior long-term institutional capacity both with leaders and organizing concepts.
6. Ensure Board self-governance.

Note the word, ensure, begins each point. One of Patterson's predecessors, Leslie Wexner, had stated their board job was "not to do things but, rather, to ensure that things get done—and to ensure that the university's resources are aligned with desired results."

A board that is responsible for several universities generally has two more duties: (1) to ensure consistency in such items as academic calendar, course numbering, and credit transfer, and (2) to monitor and exercise some control over program duplication. For example, should states with limited population have two state university colleges of engineering or six colleges of education?

It is in this latter area—proposing a curriculum or program that already exists at another university, or preventing the closing, by the board, of a duplicate program—that presidents in multi-university systems often encounter frustration. A board decision to close a college or program that may have existed for decades can put a president in a no-win situation between the board and the university's constituency—faculty, students, alumni, and community!

In this twenty-first century, universities are expected to be more entrepreneurial in their management, and there appears to be less multi-university board attention to program duplication. If a duplicate program can be efficient, the market demands it, and fees (and/or other funds) will help finance it, why not continue—or initiate—a duplicate program? If enrollment is too low for efficiency and scarce resources can be used better elsewhere, the university administration should—and is expected to—close the program (perhaps with formal board approval) and reallocate dollars. Each university's stated mission, approved by the board and appropriately differentiating it from the other state universities, should provide the major guidance. Entrepreneurial management is expected, and the freedom to exercise such management can enhance your satisfaction as president and that of your management team.

Regardless of whether your board is a one-university board or is responsible for a system of several universities, you need to work at maintaining a positive relationship with your board as a whole and with individual members. And, in a multiple-university system, that relationship includes the board staff. I suggest you figure out which members have the most influence on board direction and action. Among the nine board members that hired me as president of Kansas State, the power of two, a former legislator and chair of a financial institution, was evident. The other seven voted, of course, but the experience and force of personality of those two clearly set the board tone and direction.

In rare cases it may be that one individual essentially controls the board, and to the outsider it may be surprising who that is. Early in my SDSU deanship, President Briggs and I were called to a board meeting in Pierre and were surprised that it was held in the governor's office. The topic was a new veterinary diagnostic and research laboratory, the funds for which the livestock industry had successfully lobbied the state legislature, and planning was underway. A Washington-based consultant had urged the board to accept federal atomic energy funds he had found that could expand—*and change significantly the use of*—that laboratory. Briggs introduced me and I explained to the board why we should by-pass those federal funds and stick to the original plan. The governor said he agreed with me, there was rapid concurring board action, and the meeting adjourned.

A week later, over peas and pork chops in the home of board member Hilbert Bogue, I expressed my surprise at the meeting's location and the governor's role. Bogue explained, "The governor supports the livestock industry and he wanted to be sure the board did." Then he added, "Beyond that, when we accepted the governor's nomination to the Board, we each gave him a signed and undated letter of resignation." Through that governor's tenure, we knew who controlled the board!

Does the board tend to get involved in management—want to approve the football coach or get deeply involved in how funds or space are allocated? If that becomes a problem, Ohio State Trustee Hendricks says you need to "politely but firmly remind the board" that their role does not include administration. If, at the time of your hiring, you and the board agreed on the rules of board engagement, only a reminder should be needed.

I once had a board member call to tell me privately I should close a specific program. If that happens, I suggest two actions: (1) suggest to the member that a briefing on the topic would be appropriate for a future board agenda—and provide full program background to *all* members; and (2) have a visit with the board chair with the message, "If I am to be effective in carrying out board policy, it has to be collective policy." The chair and others of the board need to see to it that the board functions as a unit.

You can not afford to let board members get surprised on some significant university issue. You need to alert them to it before someone else does. You should be open and frank, and include the steps already planned to address the problem. If the board needs to play a role, you should outline that role.

Answer board members' questions directly and succinctly, and insist that your key staff do the same. Friend and neighbor Jim Tyler, a former Iowa regent, recalled his frustration, "When the university doesn't want you to know something—perhaps an answer to a specific question—they will bury you in details but what you really want to know is absent." He wanted "Just the facts!"

Former University of Missouri board member Edwin Turner gives this advice to a new president, "Never take a proposal to a board meeting without having sent briefing information to members, having pre-sold it to at least several, and having counted noses, those likely votes of support." His advice gives a clue to his political experience; before his board service Mr. Turner was chief of staff for the late Missouri Congressman, Jerry Litton.

Former University of Nebraska President Woody Varner was a master at scheduling board meetings at locations where members needed awareness and exposure. Meetings would be on one of the three (now four) campuses, at an out-state research and extension center, or at a regional medical facility that was cooperating with the university's medical center. Regents would see the facilities, perhaps the opportunity for expansion or a facility need, meet key staff, and hear clientele describe the university's importance to the region. Local community leaders would host a reception or luncheon. Local media would interview board members, who could extol the merits—and financial needs—of that location and the total university.

Every board member appreciates being kept posted. Periodically I sent a one- to two-page letter to members, with a copy to the board executive officer. I would include two to five succinct items, such as background on upcoming agenda items, student successes, or an example of research output. My target was a five-minute read, with attachments that could tell them more. E-mail is quick and easy, but can be over-used. Most members do not want to be buried with detail; most want attention limited to the big issues. Trustees are busy people; they prize brevity and clarity.

It is wise to get members involved in the directions you see the university needing to move. If it is an extension program to the inner city or a growing industry, take a couple board members with you to see the need and potential. Get their reaction to the external funding that can come or the broader clientele that can be served. I wanted to develop more international programs. When we were ready to propose an international trade institute and seek state funding, my dean of business and a staff member flew with me to explain the plan to several board members in their offices. That let them know how important we felt the program was. It also let them take us, on a couple occasions, to their Rotary or Lions club meeting and, in introducing us, tell their friends how valuable this program might be to the state.

When new board members are nominated, you should make immediate contact and offer any services that might be needed. (See also Chapter 56, Identify Potential Board Members.) For a system board, orientation on the board role, meeting arrangements, and reimbursement policies are likely handled by a board executive officer. If the board serves only your university, you need to see that it gets done. Do not let new board members get embarrassed on policies and procedures. Trustee Hendricks adds a point here, "Some members will have had corporate board experience, others not. See that appropriate training is provided." AGB offers workshops and conferences for trustees.

Invite new board members for a tour of the campus and some off-campus units, and introduced them to members of your management team. They need to become acquainted with the university's stated mission, vision, and goals, and be briefed on current and anticipated issues. They will have questions that need to be answered and concerns that need to be heard. Your follow-up with background information on any topic in which they express interest should be complete and timely.

It pays to find an opportunity to get new board members involved early in some university program or activity, perhaps to speak at or chair a conference. Every board member should be involved in some university events and given recognition at these events. They give their time and talent without pay; satisfaction and recognition are their reward.

As mentioned in Chapter 2, The State University Presidency, you may sometimes feel "out there all alone." When you need advice on an item, or perhaps just a solid person to talk to, I urge that you call a board member. He or she will be complimented when asked for advice. Your governing board, its chair, and other key members, should be your available and supportive "anchor."

To keep a strong and positive board relationship is, for you, a high priority. As important is your relationship with the faculty—and that is the subject of the next chapter.

CHAPTER 45

The Faculty

My wife and I were hosting faculty and their spouses for a series of open houses soon after we were settled in the president's home. Among the first at our door was a long-time professor of economics and his wife. With no little emotion, he thanked us for the invitation and added, "I've never before been in the president's home!"

The needs and desires that faculty may have, the perceptions they have of the president and other top university officers, and their response to leadership judgments and actions vary considerably among individuals. To this senior professor, being acknowledged by an invitation to the president's home was important and appreciated.

What *do* faculty seek? In preparing to draft this section, I first reviewed my own wants—and their sequence of emergence—as I considered the departments to which I would submit my short resume for an instructor's position, what I looked for in an interview visit, and the concerns that unfolded during subsequent faculty years. I then tested those items—and their sequence of emergence—against the concerns and questions raised by those I later interviewed, hired, and worked with in successive administrative posts. Following are those concerns in their approximate sequence. The first five were paramount in my early applications and interviews; the others, generally, came later:

1. Are the department, college, and university respected?
2. What is expected of me?
3. Will I have adequate facilities in which to work—lab, classroom, office.
4. Will I have supportive colleagues?
5. Will I be allowed to be creative—do my own thing within my assigned sector?
6. Do administrative processes—requisitions, reimbursement, repairs—work?
7. Is my work—and am I—noticed, respected, recognized, and appreciated?

8. Am I in the loop, kept informed of what is going on?
9. Do I have influence on what happens; do my opinions count?
10. Is my salary fair?

Your periodic review of that list of concerns may be useful. New faculty are continually being hired and others are moving along in their careers, seniority, and leadership. Salary is important, but not Number 1. Salary is negotiated at the initial appointment but, from then on, the main concern is fairness in relation to productivity and faculty rank.

The morning after we had unloaded our furniture and a couple of days before reporting for duty as Vice Chancellor at the University of Nebraska, Information Director Dick Fleming stopped by with some briefing materials. As he rose to leave he commented, "By the way, the extension home economics staff (one of my responsibilities) has just filed suit against the university regarding salary equity." Those staff obviously felt their salary levels were not fair. That suit and other issues led us rather quickly to our research statistician and a sophisticated multi-variant salary analysis. She first determined, from existing data, the degree of influence on salary of each major factor—degree, discipline, rank, years in rank, etc. That information was then used in a prediction equation to determine what the fair salary of each faculty member would be *if his or her performance were average*. Deviations from that predicted salary—up or down—then had to be justified by his or her supervisor on the basis of performance and productivity.

Your early exposure as a new president is primarily to the more senior faculty, such as leaders of the faculty senate or councils and committees, mostly associate and full professors. Salaries will be a primary topic; expressed concerns will likely be items 6 through 10, and in reverse order. They will likely ask:

1. What will you do about faculty salaries, now lagging behind peer universities?
2. Will you listen to the faculty; will you use committee input?
3. Will you be open with us; will you share information?
4. Do you respect and appreciate the diverse faculty disciplines?
5. What will you do to see that our computer system, always down for repair, is fixed? (Or other item.)

They will also want to hear your perspective on higher education and your administrative philosophy. However, listening, and perhaps some mental or written note-taking, will also be important in those early group meetings. On the salary issue, you can share what you know about peer university comparisons. Faculty leaders will appreciate that you have gathered that information. Beyond that, I suggest asking faculty leaders if they can provide what you will need to support salary increase requests, such as examples of research productivity, student success, or state-wide impact of extension programs. You need that help to build the case for increased salary appropriations.

You may ask about faculty committees. Do they serve the purpose of faculty input on key issues? Are there voids? Are there periodic reviews of deans and department heads in which faculty are involved? Are there tenure and promotion committees at the department, college, and university level? Should there be? Is committee membership generally broad and diverse? Are minorities, women, and the lower faculty ranks adequately represented? Is there sufficient turn-over for fresh input? (Councils and committees are discussed in more detail in Chapter 35.) What information do faculty members now receive from administration and what is missing? Is it timely?

Perhaps the easiest thing that a new president can insure will happen, with the help of a good information officer, is a steady flow of information to faculty and staff—perhaps a weekly electronic or printed newsletter, and as-they-happen electronic reports on governing board or legislative actions. Nothing need prevent such, but on many campuses it remains a void, simply because of inattention to the need or failure to assign a person to make it happen.

Some faculty may be concerned about a new president's discipline. If you are an engineer or chemist, will the fine arts and the social sciences be respected and appreciated? If a sociologist, will the biological and physical sciences be supported? Is there risk you will favor your own discipline in budget allocations? Some were surprised when I, an animal scientist by training, went to bat with our Kansas regents for a proposed Master of Arts degree in art. It had been turned down at least twice before my time. A *veterinarian* on the board helped me get it approved! Those with worries about my agricultural background did not consider that I might see balance and symmetry when judging animals, that I prefer low altitude flying so I can enjoy the terrace patterns on loess hills, or that I would encourage a godson through two degrees in art.

For the computer system being down, and other such issues, you will just need to listen and empathize. However, it would be wise to identify a few visible items of complaint, such as potholes at the campus entrance, the stopped clock on the central campus tower, or perhaps a library that does not open until eight a.m., and see that they get repaired or changed very quickly. You will get some valuable credit!

You should consider that the impact of every faculty interaction is magnified by those faculty members' links to colleagues, students, community friends, out-state clientele, and professional acquaintances. You—as the new president—are *the* conversation topic. You are speaking to and being observed by a far broader audience than those physically present.

Purdue Trustee John Hardin says that one of the most effective early actions of President Martin Jischke was to hold a reception for those faculty designated as "distinguished professors." According to Hardin, "By getting the best and brightest on board early, Jischke set a tone for the strategic plan that followed and the university's efforts to get better."

Throughout your presidency, you and your management team will need good faculty input and good faculty judgment, as well as faculty support. Many important judgments are made by a faculty senate or other major faculty councils and committees. Faculty will make good judgments and provide you good advice on any university issue *if they have complete information and sufficient time to debate and consider*. They are complimented when they are asked for advice, as individuals or as committees or councils.

On July 1, the first day of a fiscal year midway in my presidency, Governor John Carlin called to tell me that every state agency and university had to reduce their state fund budget four percent. Since spring legislature adjournment tax receipts and projections for the fiscal year had dropped sharply. We already had our fiscal year operating budget in place and for Kansas State that cutback would be several million dollars. Provost Koeppe and I pulled together an ad hoc committee—leadership of faculty and student senate and a couple selected deans and department heads—for advice. We devoted two or three afternoons to discussing options and developing a set of university-wide guidelines for the reductions. That process not only led us to reasonable actions, each person involved left the last meeting feeling he or she had played an important role. And their peers—faculty, other department heads and other deans—were more prepared and willing to accept and carry out the budget adjustments.

Carrying out those budget adjustments was the more difficult task—terminating some part-time staff, reducing travel allocations, combining a few classes, and deciding which intended equipment purchases could be postponed. When that job was done, to recognize and express appreciation for their handling that task, we invited the deans and department heads and their spouses to a backyard barbecue. Although budget reduction had not been fun, we could not help but notice some feeling of "esprit de corps" in the group, a subtle expression of "Together, we got it done!"

In faculty recruitment, especially for senior faculty and department heads, look not only at knowledge, skills, and experience, but also at capacity for judgment on broad academic issues. The same applies for promotion and tenure decisions. Among the most important days in the life of a university are the days when new tenure-track faculty are hired and the days that decisions are made to grant promotion and tenure. Those days' decisions will determine the quality and reputation of your university 10, 20, and 30 years hence. In regard to those decisions to hire, promote, or grant, I suggest the principle, "*If in doubt, don't!*"

Another important day is the day you, and perhaps others, appoint key people to major university council or committee positions. Those appointments will determine the wisdom and value of the council and committee decisions and judgments on which, in many cases, you will depend.

CHAPTER 46

The Students

t was a total surprise when, at a Friday Board of Regents meeting, a member moved that the student union at one of our sister universities be allowed to sell beer. Beer sales in university unions were not uncommon in other states but, in conservative Kansas, the topic had never been openly discussed. In seconds, the motion was amended to include all campuses and the motion passed. (It was never disclosed who or what triggered that action.)

I called to alert my vice president for student affairs, Chet Peters. His quick response, "We should let the student union board decide if they want to sell beer." Though beer was flowing by Saturday noon in the unions on at least two campuses, our union board held back, decided to ask for student input. The union board then debated the issue for several weeks and eventually made the judgment, no beer sales in our union. "We may like beer," some members said, "but Aggieville is the better place for beer sales."

Student leaders, as with faculty leaders, will make good judgments when they have complete information, time to discuss and debate, and responsibility for both the judgment and the consequences. Sustained good relationships between you, as a new president (or the total administration) and the student body depend on three factors:

1. Student perceptions of your (and fellow administrators') respect for and interest in them. Respect and interest have to be real; students are not fooled. Perception can be enhanced, though, perhaps by scheduling an overnight in a residence hall, joining students for lunch in the commons, or a travel to an away game with your pep band. Perceptions can be enhanced more if a Collegian photographer happens to be on hand.

2. Student affairs staff and college deans/associate deans who work closely with student leaders and lead effective academic advising systems in their colleges.

3. Thoughtful and mature faculty chosen to advise the student senate, student newspaper or radio station, departmental clubs, club sports, and other student groups.

The adviser to Kansas State's crew (rowing) club chose my second day in the presidency to publicly blast "the administration." He said he needed more funds for crew and threatened to resign. He was a hard-working young man who had built a lot of enthusiasm. Somehow he had put together some shells and he and his club members had fixed up a small headquarters and storage building on the banks of nearby Tuttle Creek Lake. The next morning brought a phone call from one of his patrons, a woman well into her 80s. Her message was direct, "You are the new president; DO something for these young people!"

The good thing for me was that I had Vice President Peters, under whom club sports were organized. He knew the adviser well and had fielded his outbursts before. Most important, Peters was deeply respected by students, as well as by student organization advisers, for always listening, considering options, and making judgments that would stand the test of time. He would handle that problem, visit and empathize with the adviser, and assure him and crew members that their hard work and concerns were recognized. And, maybe that adviser would mature a bit in the process.

As an associate dean, a decade before returning as president, I had established a rather strong academic advising system in my college. My successor, Carroll Hess and his associate, David Mugler, had continued that system and its history was reasonably well known among faculty, but generations of students had come and gone and I was dealing with students who did not know me. I met weekly with the student senate and student body presidents and accepted invitations from department clubs, residence halls, and other student groups. Fraternities and sororities often invited my wife and me to dinner and short discussions in their living rooms often followed.

Both my wife and I are comfortable with student groups and they with us. Two students rang our doorbell about 10:30 one Saturday night to invite me to accompany them downtown to Swanny's, a bakery that shifted from their front door daytime cakes and rolls trade to a nighttime backdoor line up of students hungry for twists and bismarks. Such involvement was not uncommon—and part of the "spontaneity" we enjoyed in working with university students. With student-oriented college deans, good student club advisers, and my dedicated student affairs staff, student relations seemed to be in good shape. But problems do emerge.

I was at lunch with our southeast extension staff in Emporia when I received a call about a planned four-o'clock student protest outside my office. Could I be on hand? The protest was designed to build interest in joining that caravan to Topeka and the legislature on the Nichols Gym issue, described in Chapter 40.

At four o'clock, I was on the south steps of Anderson Hall where the organizers had a microphone set up; a few dozen students were gathering. I noticed the organizers huddling beside me, then one confessed, "We have a problem. Tickets for a fabulous concert go on sale at the union in just a few minutes. Most of the students we expected are in the ticket line. Can we delay our protest until five?"

"No problem." I answered, and turned to go inside to my office. At that, I heard a "boo" from the small crowd. I grabbed the mike, "I am here, ready to both listen and comment, but your leaders want to delay this until five so you can go buy concert tickets. I will be here at five and ready to listen."

Two women students followed me into my office; they wanted to tell me personally why they disagreed with razing most of the Nichols shell. One, though, could not hold her excitement at the whole thing, "I am so glad this is happening—the protest, I mean! There were so many protests when my sister was here and I was afraid I'd go all the way through college and there'd never be one!"

With the help of Director of Residence, Tom Frith, and Peters, students in our residence hall system helped resolve some of the financial residue of the university's athletics problems. In hiring a new football coach, we had established there would no longer be an "athletic dorm." (Athletes would be dispersed in other housing options, and have a "training table" in one of the commons.) The athletic dorm structure, though relatively new, was in bad shape, on foundation-owned land, heavily mortgaged, and the athletics department was committed to paying off the mortgage. I had convinced our board that the state (university) could accept mortgaged property as a gift from the foundation, and our department of residence would manage the building.

One problem remained: Tens of thousands of dollars were needed to restore the building to decent condition and the only money in sight was a fund set aside to update some residence hall recreation rooms, a project long planned. Frith put the issue to his residence hall student leaders and staff. They discussed and debated and, in time, reached the judgment, "It needs to be done. We'll just put off our recreation room updating a year or two." Given the information and the responsibility, students will make good judgments, perhaps judgments sorely needed.

My secretary, wearing a big smile, came into my office to say a couple of students wanted to see me. She stepped aside and in they came with a donut and a cup of hot tea. (My affinity for donuts was rather well known.) That morning, the Collegian had rather severely and, I thought, unfairly roasted me on some athletics issue. The students did not mention that, they "just thought I might enjoy a donut and a cup of tea." Nothing could have been as effective in wiping away the sting of that Collegian piece. I did not ask, but I have a strong suspicion that one thoughtful faculty member may have been discussing that Collegian article with some students and might have suggested, "If you guys agree with the president, you might find a way to let him know that." Such are the rewards of working with top faculty and top students.

A good administration—student relationship is also dependent on the behavior and demonstrated interest of every member of your management team, as well as instructors, academic advisers, and office staff. But you, as president, set the pattern.

CHAPTER

The Media

Former Michigan State President McPherson, with whom I worked in USAID, offers positive advice, "Let the media help you. They will respond to good actions." He also reminds, "Faculty and staff read the local paper. It is a good way to communicate with them!" An experienced information officer is one of your most valuable staff, and needs to be a part of your inner circle, involved and fully informed. That information officer must develop good relations with key media, be available, and be reliable.

As I was departing for the presidency at Kansas State, UNL Chancellor Jim Zumberge cautioned me about over-reacting to unfair or inaccurate reporting. "Remember, today's newspapers are used to wrap tomorrow's fish." It was good advice. Though the sting may remain, most readers will have forgotten the issue by morning. Be cautious about writing letters to the editor. If there are serious factual errors that must be rebutted, your information officer should make a judgment as to who should write a correction. If you are sufficiently incensed to write such a letter, it might be well to write it—but then drop it in the file (marked "drafted but not sent") or waste basket. Such a letter delivered and printed would just extend the story or give some the perception that "there must be something to the issue." SDSU Provost Peterson says it well, "Don't make a 10-day story out of a brief newspaper item."

"Do good things and then tell the people about them" is the basic rule of public relations. But, problems do appear and some actions are controversial. For those, there is another rule: "The one who gets their story out first usually wins." When problems arise, there is no merit in trying to avoid the media. Get the facts together and the story out. If some necessary facts are not yet known, the statement should say so. In the first release, or as soon thereafter as possible, list the steps the institution has taken or will take—staff or committee review, or other—to address the problem.

How about a staff member who goes to the media with a complaint about some "foolish" decision by a department head, dean, or you, the president? How about a "whistle blower," one who goes to the media with a financial or other irregularity in one of the top offices? How should they be handled—with the media and with the accuser?

These are two different types of issues. In regard to the latter, if it is credible and involves you, or, if you have been informed and refuse to investigate or otherwise address the issue, media exposure is justified and the "whistle blower" should be defended. (I found in federal agencies that an agency's general counsel is the more common recipient of such complaints or accusations; it served that function as well as being the legal adviser to line officers. That office would investigate and take the findings to the appropriate higher level; perhaps negative media attention would be avoided. Such an office or arrangement is worthy of university consideration.)

In the former case, however, my well-communicated policy to staff in the university, federal agency, or business has been that any decision I make can be appealed to me to reconsider or to my superior. (If the latter, "I'll make an appointment for you and go with you or you can go alone—your choice.") I expect the same for the decisions of a department head, dean, vice president, or provost—any decision they make can be appealed. And for any decision I may make as president, an appeal to the chair of the board is not improper. But, for a staff member to go public *without* a request for reconsideration or an appeal in some form is out of bounds.

I was therefore surprised to read in our local paper a complaint by one of our planning office staff about the design of a drive and handicap parking area for our auditorium. The lack of such had been a long-time campus and community problem—the auditorium had been built in a crowded spot and without vehicle access. After many meetings by auditorium personnel, planning staff, and others, the "least undesirable" option had been generally agreed to, and then approved by our facilities vice president, Gene Cross, and me. Cross was a no-nonsense guy and recommended the complaining staff member, on an annual contract, be told his contract would not be renewed, and I concurred.

A justified decision, but bad timing. The nonrenewal became the next day's story! And, we had made an earlier error. Since the lack of a convenient drive and parking area had been a long-time and well-discussed campus and community thorn, the university should have put out a media release on *the afternoon the decision was made*, including the problem, the several options, the chosen solution, and the reasons.

For any significant presentation you may make, off-campus or on, there should be a media release. A speech to a service club or an alumni club in the far corner of the state is significant in that community. A local reporter may cover the talk, but the odds are high the writer will also lift some items from the release. Nearby media may also use the release; more people will read or hear the media coverage than will be in the physical audience. If, upon accepting a speaking invitation, you give your information staff the three or four points you intend to cover, staff will have plenty of time to put together both the presentation—if that is expected—and the release. It is a good routine to follow!

Should you try to influence the campus newspaper or radio station? Football Coach Jim Dickey called me late one night to ask that I try to get our Collegian editor to kill a story about the antics of one of his players. I empathized with Coach Dickey, but declined. The story appeared—and the story died. Your best influence on a campus newspaper or radio station is to insure it has a mature and respected adviser and an editorial board with defined responsibility. Should you—or someone on your behalf—try to throttle or unduly influence a story, *that* may become the story.

How about news conferences? My judgment is "only when warranted," such as national recognition of student achievements, a major research breakthrough, an extraordinarily large donation, a serious student health problem, or a new athletic director or coach in a major sport. In a large university, weekly sessions for media by the university information officer may be helpful, but regular news conferences by the president can become dull, predictable, and poorly attended.

What about a weekly column or three- to five-minute radio/TV spot? It is a rare president that can do such well. Though these can be good exposures for the university, unless you have the voice or an especially good writer, and are willing to devote the time such requires, both you and the university are better off letting others do it. Beyond that, such regular appearance risks over-exposure, a factor of concern in any public position. As president, you do not need steady media exposure and are likely better off without it. A faculty member who had been a friend since our college days commented during my third year in the presidency, "Things must be going well; I've not seen your name in the paper for several weeks!"

A tip to your information officer: Do not overlook small-town radio or weekly and suburban newspapers. It is easy to focus on major media outlets, metropolitan papers, and TV. But those local outlets have very loyal readers and listeners. Most are short on staff and odds are high they will use about anything from the university that is credible and with any chance of local interest.

CHAPTER 48

The Community

After a hard-fought Homecoming football victory and the goalposts had been pulled down, hundreds of students flocked to the pubs in Aggieville and beer flowed. By 9 o'clock that evening the pub crowds had spilled onto the street, there were a few fights, some store and car windows were broken, and benches smashed. Monday morning, a pub owner and some Aggieville merchants contacted one of my staff to urge a meeting with student leaders in our student union to talk about how to avoid another episode of that type. We would never decline a meeting to talk over a problem, but Mike Johnson, my assistant, suggested the student union was not the place, "The problem generated in the Aggieville pubs, not on campus, and the meeting should be in Aggieville." Mike was right; the public focus should be on Aggieville, not on the university.

Business communities—retails shops, apartment owners, dentists, optometrists, pubs, auto dealers, restaurants, and certainly bankers—thrive on student numbers. With university growth there is more business, more cash flow, and more sales and real estate taxes paid. But, there are also conflicts. Dozens of student and faculty cars daily lined residential streets near our campus. Most residents just considered this a part of university reality, but we had some intense complaints from neighbors of fraternities and sororities. Most of their houses were built decades earlier, before students brought cars to campus, and house expansions intensified the problem. Tuttle Creek Lake, just three miles from the campus, made it worse. Fraternity members gave parking lot priority to their boats—and even more cars were on the streets!

City ordinances are the legal vehicle for regulating street parking but, especially with more commuting students and faculty, stadium lots are now commonly open to student, faculty, and even visitor parking, except on game days. Student fees and/or university funds usually subsidize the cost of shuttles to central campus.

The Omaha campus of the University of Nebraska, extending along the south side of Dodge Street, is beautiful and at least twice the size it was a couple decades ago. But, the west half of that campus came only with considerable community pain. Before campus expansion it was the site of some of Omaha's most beautiful old family homes. To accommodate rising enrollment in a rapidly growing metropolitan area, university regents, UNO administration, and foundation staff incurred a good bit of wrath. In most cases, the foundation was the real estate purchaser, negotiating and holding the property until state or other funds were available. And, at this writing, more pain is ahead. Omaha's continued population growth and UNO's resultant expansion demands even more space. Expansion to the south, into more residential areas, is planned.

Almost every Sunday morning during my associate dean days at Kansas State, a fellow worshipper accosted me in the church foyer to complain about the flies and smell from the university dairy across the street from their home. Of course, the dairy and its cows had been there for decades before she and her husband bought the land and built their home. By the time I returned to the campus as president, the cows and other animal units were gone, to new facilities a mile north of the campus and at a cost of several million dollars. But the town had also grown, home builders were scouting for development land, and the most attractive site, hills overlooking the town and Tuttle Creek Lake, was several hundred acres of hills *just beyond those new animal units!*

I could see the problem ahead—spring and summer south breeze from the dairy cows, beef research feedlots, and the swine and poultry units wafting over a couple hundred new homes. And, more complaints every Sunday morning at church! Fortunately, the land was owned by two sisters and they would not sell. But, within a year, both died and the land would be on the market. To me there was but one option for the university. Home builders were not pleased, but our foundation stepped in and bought the land.

As university president, you can and should be one of the "thought leaders" of the community—and your deans, department heads, and certain faculty should also play key roles. Though there is political risk on some issues, you can stimulate thought, identify opportunities, and provide important support to local community, business, and cultural developments. Presidents—and their spouses—can serve effectively on community boards and commissions. My wife was a valiant member of a local hospital board during the time the community's two hospitals were trying to hammer out a joint working relationship. Her respect in the community and her ability to listen to all sides helped keep discussions on an even keel.

Local residents appreciate an invitation to the president's campus home, and we included several at any opportunity to interact with university staff or guests—receptions for new faculty, alumni boards, regents, commencement parties, or visiting dignitaries. Because my wife served on the local civic theatre board, we also hosted several social and fund-raising events for theatre supporters.

If the local chamber of commerce or development board invites you to designate a staff member to an ad hoc spot on their board, by all means do it. University leadership should never miss an opportunity for personal communication in the community. Your university liaison will learn of new plans or problems that may impact the university, perhaps dispel some unfounded university rumor, or maybe even intercept some inappropriate staff activity. I was to learn years later that a few months before my arrival as president, a newly hired football coach had convened a group of local business people to explain that he needed cash in order to recruit top talent. A sizeable group responded; they wanted to help, and they gave him considerable cash. Of course, that and other of his behavior brought conference and NCAA sanctions. Could more campus–main street communication have somehow prevented that meeting?

How about the president serving on the boards of local banks, insurance companies, or other businesses? I was warned not to; the business competitiveness in the community was so intense that several advised that I should not identify with one vs. others. However, I thereby missed some communication opportunities.

Advice to a new president? Get to know people. Do a lot of listening. Keep communication open. Keep enrollment expanding and football teams winning. Challenge community leaders when that is needed. And, buy every adjacent lot or tract of land that is available and for which there may be future need.

PART VIII

Tending Yourself

When you are appointed to a university presidency every person is your friend and supporter, or wants to be. However, about every major decision you make can risk some friendships and some support. As in any public leadership position, with successive decisions, "friends can dissipate and enemies accumulate."

A presidency, given the constant demands on your campus time plus considerable travel, can be physically exhausting.

Conflicting demands and priorities of constituent groups as well the need to support and guide ambitious and aggressive members of your team can be emotionally trying.

To maintain political support, internal and external, and the physical and emotional energy you need to lead the university and also maintain your family relationships, you need to look after yourself.

Here are some suggestions.

CHAPTER  49

Keep a Sense of Humor

ending over the water fountain near my office, I caught a conversation among three girls on an adjacent bench. Oblivious of me, they were pouring out complaints about the residence hall food service. I wanted to hear more, and remained bent over the fountain. One said she had complained to staff and got no response. The second echoed that. The third, in mock courage and in a voice I thought I recognized, "Well, I'll just go down and talk to Duane about that!"

I could not resist, raised my head, turned to her, and asked, "Is there something I can help you with?" When the shock and laughter subsided, she offered, "My dad told me that someday my mouth would get me in trouble!"

One of my friends, talking about my presidential authority, suggested, "Authority goes with rank—and the president is the rankest!" Though you must take your job seriously, you cannot afford to take yourself seriously. You need to be able to laugh at yourself.

There is plenty of humor in a university—faculty battles, bureaucracy, state regulations, curriculum debates, fraternity or residence hall antics, and even excuses for overtime parking. What one does not encounter in issues that come to your office will be found in the student or the state's newspapers—letters to the editor, misquotes, or the sports columns. Even those that sting will give you a smile in later years. I suggest clipping and saving a few.

A good sense of humor helps you stay healthy. It can also defuse a tense discussion or situation.

CHAPTER

Stay Healthy

As I was preparing to leave for a weekend at our farm, my staff walked in with a gift—an axe handle festooned with a red bow. It had been a stressful week, climaxed when I learned our security staff had towed Foundation Chair Al Hostetler's car from a time-limited spot near the student union. My staff figured I would break an axe handle cutting brush that weekend.

A university presidency brings plenty of stress; in some cases, mental health may be more at risk than physical health. You will have many pressures, some directly opposite others. You will have successes and frustrations, wins and losses. Pressures can build, be "all consuming," and sap your emotional strength or stability. Frustrations may overshadow, in time and in your mind, your many successes.

During my time at Kansas State, our faculty had several cooperative research and education programs with the Menninger Foundation Clinic, then of Topeka and now of Houston. From Menninger materials, I drew a set of rules for maintaining good mental health and included them in presentations to leadership workshops. Adapted to university administration, they are:

1. *Have multiple sources of gratification*. In addition to the university, they might be woodworking and music. Or playing bridge and restoring an antique car. If you have a bad streak in one, you can find satisfaction in another. At least one of those sources should be one you can turn to any day or any time, and where the yielding of satisfaction is totally under your control.
2. *Recognize your assets and your limitations*. Have a reasonably accurate picture of yourself and like what you see. Do those things you are good at and have the time to do well; charge others with handling those things better handled by them.
3. *Be flexible*. Stand your ground when you know you are right, but be willing to compromise when that is best for the university. Recognize there are different ways of handling an issue.

4. *Stay physically healthy.* Get enough sleep, eat only a portion of those large banquet meals, and get some intensive physical exercise on a regular basis. Not only may it lengthen your life, an intensive workout—jogging, swimming, lifting weights, etc.—can be a source of immediate pride and satisfaction.

5. *Develop friendships.* You will have friends within the university; you need some good friends outside the institution, people with "no axe to grind," and whose status or future is outside your realm of influence.

6. *Associate with positive people.* Value the people who see a problem as an opportunity, who focus on solutions.

For me, racquetball served several functions—intense exercise, release of emotions, regular time with an off-campus friend, and some satisfaction with every point scored.

CHAPTER 5

Behave

A university presidency is a "heady position." One can slip into an attitude that any presidential behavior is justified or accepted, that "I can get by." More than one president has been professionally destroyed or damaged, and the institution at least temporarily scarred, by careless or improper behavior. In a recent five-year period, I noted unfortunate instances of college or university presidential behavior:

1. One who was an alcoholic. Deans took turns accompanying him to events to control his drinking, and to drive him home when they could not.
2. One who became romantically involved with the spouse of a board member.
3. One who was an active party to changing the course grade of a star athlete, to maintain the athlete's eligibility.
4. One who provided false travel and entertainment reimbursement claims. The money derived was "peanuts."
5. Even one discovered to be cultivating marijuana in his college-provided home!

A president can also be a tempting target for a charge, or at least a strong rumor, of sexual harassment or other impropriety. Do not take a chance. Be prudent and cautious. Be sure that all of your compensation is authorized and all reimbursement requests are well documented. Do not let staff by-pass or, in their effort to make your life easier, encourage you to by-pass established regulations and policies.

Do not get involved in any activity that would violate or that would imply toleration of violations in athlete recruitment or eligibility. The same holds for donations to your foundation, especially requests for handling funds in ways that violate evident IRS regulations (such as a scholarship fund for the exclusive use of the donor's grandchildren). Do not let a donor, board member, or political leader talk you into improper actions.

Be sure that you have close colleagues with a "true compass" and loyal enough that they are willing to say, "Don't do that!" I also suggest that you follow the "newspaper test": take no action and make no decision that you would not be willing to see fully reported in tomorrow's newspaper.

CHAPTER

Keep a Journal

I n later years—or perhaps before that—you will appreciate the journal and you may need it. I offer four reasons for you—or anyone who has the privilege of working with enthusiastic students, creative faculty, competitive coaches, and so many university friends—to keep a journal:

1. It can be a record of your observations, impressions, perhaps commitments, and delegation or charges to staff. It may provide bases for later judgments.
2. Dated and initialed, it can be credible documentation in cases of disagreement or legal action.
3. It will help you with a written or oral history of your presidency or of the institution.
4. You may want to write an autobiography or at least a summary of your presidential and life experiences and, certainly, some of the humor.

What should be in a journal? Include what you think is important, especially dates, names, and major content of conversations. General impressions of a days' events or circumstances may well be of interest later.

I suggest keeping a journal simple and chronological; you will more likely do it. It can be hand-written notes on each day's calendar or in a bound notebook. It can be dictated, or typed on a laptop. If dictated, it should get transcribed. If on a laptop, I suggest printing out a hard copy. Computers can crash and old discs may not be easily read on later equipment.

Seven years after leaving SDSU, I was called back to Sioux Falls to testify in court on a case of alleged salary discrimination. My successor brought the office files for the case. It was comforting to see and to offer the court a series of transcriptions, all dated and signed, of the conversations I had had with the plaintiff. SDSU won the case.

When odds are high for disagreement, formal appeals, or legal action, details of every conversation should be recorded, dated, and signed or initialed. Such can be a section of a journal or a separate document, but a date and signature or initial are essential for total credibility. A rule to all my office staff has been, in regard to any item prepared or received, "If it doesn't walk, date it!"

More than one university case involving personnel actions or patent rights has been lost because university witnesses could only say, in court or in arbitration, "My memory is that. . . ." One's memory may be superb, but my lawyer daughter reminds me that, in court or arbitration, it is of limited value.

One more point. Keep (fully identified and dated) some of the photographs that record major events, interactions with key colleagues, university supporters and campus guests. They will become more and more valuable to you as years elapse. Further, a university presidency "ages" some people; you might want a reminder of what you looked like when you started the job!.

CHAPTER

Develop a Kitchen Cabinet

Every university has some steady and sincere friends, inside and out, who can be depended on for quiet and considered advice, judgment, and feedback. As a new president, find a few. They will be the type who will not feel the need to tell others they are "close to the president." They will keep your confidence. And, they will give you their time when you need it.

Your administrative structure should be respected, for both information and actions. But no matter how good that structure nor how capable the people in it, it has its limits as an information and opinion vehicle. Each person's perspective is limited and information gets filtered.

You will sometimes need distant and unbiased observations and thoughts—from people whose status or responsibility is not involved. Such will not only help you, it can help your administrative team, through which most decisions will be made and actions taken.

The term 'cabinet' may mislead. Visits you may have with the people I suggest will usually be one-on-one and as you or they feel the need. Contact may be rare; it may be often. Among such people may be a state or community leader; a local businessperson, or a senior staff or faculty member. There may be a corporate leader, a retired legislator, or former governor. Among those extremely helpful to me were a National Guard officer, a metropolitan editor, a retired dean, a local banker, a long-time research station superintendent, an information officer in one of our colleges, a former alumni association president, and a high school teacher.

You should not overlook members of the administrative team on issues outside their sphere of responsibility. Each may play the kitchen cabinet role in other areas. Especially, you should not overlook a president or other administrator whom you worked under at another university. He or she will be complimented and will have your interests at heart. More than once I used one or two as sounding boards and for advice.

CHAPTER 54

Insulate Yourself from Predictable Splatter

Y ou can predict some splatter (public criticism, media attention, internal flak, or a late night phone call) from about any decision on most of the following.

1. Intercollegiate athletics: coaches, athletic directors, conference relationships.
2. Building demolitions. "Can it not be saved?"
3. Program eliminations or college or department restructuring.
4. Community relationships. Student behavior, on-street parking, traffic flow.
5. New building priorities or their planned sites. "Why that one and why there?"
6. "Off the wall" behaviour in the classroom or writings by some faculty member.

Actions and decisions in any one of these areas may bring an outpouring of emotion and disagreement. Media attention can be unduly heavy. Media thrive on debate; debate attracts readers, radio listeners, and TV viewers.

In many of these issues, you should give yourself some insulation, some distance from the debate. You can still be the final arbiter or decision-maker, but you are usually best served—and the issue may be best served—by another of your team, a committee, or a combination thereof taking the lead in handling a contentious issue. They may be charged to make a decision, which may or may not be appealed to you, or to make a recommendation for your consideration. Their involvement, the time that elapses during their work, and the consequential public or internal exposure lets all parties more fully understand the issues and vent their emotions. Much of the splatter dissipates.

Personnel termination or reassignment can also bring splatter. If the reason is clear, a quick and quiet resignation or reassignment can sometimes be achieved without undue publicity. The public has little concern for most internal cases. In athletics, however, and perhaps in an area under current media scrutiny, nothing can be done without full media attention. Privacy laws and regulations must be considered, of course, but if there is not rather full exposure of the problem and the reason for reassignment or termination, interested public may have difficulty accepting the action. A full review of circumstances and issues by the athletic council, an appointed committee, or an employed investigator or auditor may give the exposure and acceptance that is needed to minimize splatter when the action is taken.

When Michigan State was accused by the NCAA of serious football recruiting violations, President McPherson brought in an outside lawyer to investigate and issue the findings. Not only was McPherson protected from most of the splatter that the findings and recommended actions caused, he was commended for his leadership in seeing to it that the issue was fully investigated.

Too much insulation can also lead to criticism. "Are you not willing to make a decision? Are problems never resolved? Why keep faculty, staff, or alumni unsettled?"

There is a balance. Your many publics want decisions made, but they also want your political strength preserved for the next issues that will certainly come.

CHAPTER

Fill Your Bucket

Most of your presidential time will be devoted to planning strategy, charging and challenging, making personnel or program judgments, lobbying board members and perhaps legislators, and cultivating donors. You will be coaching and counseling, tapping your skills and experiences, "pouring from your bucket" of internal resources. You need to take some time to "fill your bucket."

You might read biographies of business, political, and university leaders—see how they handled colleagues, issues, and problems. You might broaden your perspective with historical novels. You should keep alert to new books on societal change or organization management. I also suggest you spend some time with inspirational leadership and "positive thinking" books; such will offset some of the negativism a president invariably encounters. If on tape or CD, you can listen to these while driving, flying, or jogging.

I suggest that you identify three to five journals that should come to your desk so you can scan the Contents and the articles that appeal. Consider which of the national or regional meetings offer the most in helping you understand and do your job. At those meetings, I urge that you go to dinner or spend an evening with selected counterparts, persons with whom you can share experiences and ideas.

I also suggest that you periodically meet for a couple hours at a mutual location or an hour on the phone with a board member, a senior counterpart, a former president, or with a member of your kitchen cabinet—one you can always count on for a good idea or renewed confidence.

Do not let "your bucket" get empty.

CHAPTER

Identify Potential Board Members

In the business world, a corporate CEO, often also the board chair, plays a major role in choosing new board members. A board committee may also recruit and forward nominations, but much deference is given to the CEO's preference. State university board members, however, are commonly nominated by the governor and confirmed by the state senate. Some are elected by the public or chosen by specific groups. Should you play a role in that identification and selection process?

I suggest an active role, but exercised quietly and with prudence. You need to think seriously about who would be good for higher education, your institution, and your goals. You can solicit their interest and can suggest their names for consideration by the governor. You should.

Where board members are chosen by voters, you can encourage good people to run. Where members are chosen to represent a group, such as an alumni association, you can encourage good people to express interest and can suggest they be considered by the group. You should.

You or other of your staff can provide background and information to the potential member as they prepare for election or for an interview with the governor. That should be done.

It is proper for you to do these things. Higher education needs strong and positive policy-makers. You will know some outstanding potential board members, and will have friends who know more, people whose services would benefit your university or system and higher education as a whole.

In all such efforts, just be prudent and cautious.

CHAPTER

Take Some Credit;
Give More

I was consulting on a university campus and took time to hear a major political figure who would be introduced, according to the program, by the university president. The president's assistant appeared, welcomed the audience, and introduced the president with a ten-minute recitation of his extraordinary achievements. The main speaker was eventually introduced by the president, but had been given a tough act to follow.

How much credit should a president take—or be given by immediate staff?

As president, you will get the blame for problems; should you not get some credit for the good things that happen? For increased appropriations, enrollment growth, a winning debate or sports team, or new and needed programs, should you not be given credit? You certainly will not have written the appropriations bills, recruited all the students, coached the teams, or drafted the new curriculum, but you may have set the pattern or may have chosen and guided the person who did or guided the team member who guided the person who did.

How much credit should you be given in publications, speeches, or introductions, either by staff—or claimed in your speeches? This is a delicate issue, but important to your continued leadership strength and not to be ignored.

I see a university presidency as midway between that of a private sector CEO and a politician seeking re-election. The book cited earlier, *Good to Great*, gives consistent evidence that CEOs of those corporations who became "great" gave most of the credit to others, especially their employees and administrative team. In contrast, a governor or senator and their proxies, during a re-election campaign, will claim that on about every issue that may interest the audience, the candidate has recommended, co-sponsored, introduced, voted for, or signed legislation that supports. Unabashedly, voters are assured that their world is better because of what the candidate did and that re-election for two, four, or six more years will make their world even better.

University presidents who have focused on building and rewarding others during their careers are more comfortable with the modest behavior commended in *Good to Great*. You can be embarrassed and even ridiculed if a publication or an introduction is largely a "puff piece" for you. It is not good for the university. Or, the reverse may prevail—no mention of things that your decisions, determination, or foresight brought about. That is not good for the university – or for you.

One thing is clear to me. I have never seen a university or a university president harmed by the president giving generous credit to others—faculty, staff, department heads, deans, vice-presidents, provosts, alumni, donors, and individual friends and supporters! A cabinet officer I knew well was among the most revered by his staff and his clientele, during and for many years following his service. At every opportunity, in public presentations or in staff meetings, he expressed admiration and appreciation for the good work of his agency heads, assistant secretaries, and career staff.

By his giving credit, his audience gave *him* credit.

CHAPTER

Prepare for
Post-Presidential Years

You may, in time, move on to another presidency. You may retire from this presidency or you may seek and accept another challenge. Regardless of your age when you leave the presidency, your future years should be more than golf or hiking and the weekly service club meeting. Your skills and breadth of interest—and, perhaps, the stature you hold as a former university president—will make you valuable in a profession, in entrepreneurship, or as a volunteer. Society, government, and communities need able and experienced people with your skills and experience.

Also, we live life but once. So many different experiences are available to a former university leader, experiences that can challenge, reward and, especially, make life interesting. There are places to live, people to meet and work with, problems to solve, needs to serve, and satisfactions to experience.

Dr. James Hilton, the president under whom I served as a faculty member at Iowa State, returned to North Carolina, where he had earlier served as dean, to lead a major commodity organization. My predecessor at Kansas State, Dr. James McCain, moved directly to the governor's cabinet. He performed valuable and rewarding service as Secretary of the Kansas Department of Labor. Following retirement as dean of pharmacy at SDSU, my friend and former golf partner, Dr. Ray Hopponen, spent a year filling in for pharmacists across the state when they needed a vacation from their one-person shop. After that, in his late 60s, he joined the research staff of a veterinary pharmaceutical company and had a productive second career.

I have tried to follow their examples. My post-presidential experiences in two federal departments, program review and consulting in a about two dozen countries, and helping organize new businesses have exposed both my wife and me to many cultures (Washington, as well as international), kept us on a steep learning curve, and continue to provide endless satisfaction.

Depending on your background and interests, you might help fill knowledge, leadership, and skill voids in inner cities, rural communities, public schools, a private business, a professional or industry organization, or government. If you have considered administration a detour from your profession and want to return to that profession, keep in touch. Regularly read professional journals; teach a class in the discipline, keep your hand in some research, or do some writing. Take time for some professional meetings and seminars, and regularly join professional colleagues for lunch.

If your goal following university leadership is a private sector, I suggest investing selectively in that sector or seeking membership on a corporate board. You might attend selected seminars in the Business College and maintain subscriptions to a financial journal and the journal in your target business sector.

If you are interested in a political appointment or elective office, lay the groundwork, cultivate the relationships needed, get to know state central committee members of your political party, and establish a record of at least modest financial donations. It is best to avoid visible party identification and to stay away from party rallies. For a state university president, there are too many risks; presidents need to work with and have support from leaders of both parties, both in the state and in Washington.

A long tenure as president is not guaranteed. Nor may you desire it. I decided early in my life there was one thing I did not want—a gold watch for years of service in the same spot. I put a limit of 10 years on my presidency.

Follow the Boy Scout motto, "Be prepared."

PART IX

The Closing Acts

During your presidency, you will receive satisfaction from many quarters. No matter what the length of your service, the years will go by rapidly. Savor them. But, at some point, you will leave that important, respected, and rewarding office. When that time comes, there will be some specific obligations that need to be performed, obligations to the university, to your administrative team, to faculty and staff, to other supporters, to your successor, and—to yourself. With the aid of others, George Washington had drafted a "farewell address" six months before the end of his first term.[34] It was put away when he agreed to the second term, but it was pulled out in May of 1796, updated and revised. There were many drafts. Though not given orally as an address, and that was never Washington's intent, it was published in newspapers all across the young country. It is worth reading.

The university needs for its archives some comprehensive summary of your presidency. There should be a record of the key issues, challenges, and accomplishments—initiated curriculums and other programs, major construction, enrollment, faculty and staff growth, university recognition among its peers, contributions to the state's economy and society, faculty recognition, and other. It should also include your assessment of university opportunities and challenges ahead. A capable information staff should take leadership of this task early and have generous input from you and others. And, it should be published in some form.

You should write notes of appreciation to members of your administrative team, key faculty, staff, and student leaders. You should send appreciation to members of the governing board with whom you have worked and to certain others who may have been especially helpful and supportive during your tenure—key alumni, legislators, governors and staff, state-wide organizations, and local community leaders.

Chapter 35 mentions the value of a departing president opening the way for a successor to structure administrative and advisory councils as they may wish by thanking and "dismissing" existing groups. You should do that for your successor! Also, you should, in thanking immediate staff, remind them that your successor's administrative structure and pattern of delegation may be different from yours.

Then, I suggest, pack your bags and get out of town—for at least a year. A couple of the most frustrated people I have known have been former university presidents who stayed around to watch their faculty and townspeople pour accolades on their successor and read in the local media all the residual problems that new person faces.

If you have accepted another presidency or other position, you may be gone a few days early. If retiring, you should have made sure you have a place to go and a job you need to do—pay or no pay. You may have talked about "a rocking chair," but it is a rare former president that will use one for more than a day.

NOTES

1. Eisenhower, Milton S. 1974. *The President is Calling.* Doubleday & Co., Inc., Garden City, New York. p. 151.

2. President's Report. 2003–2004. University of Virginia, Charlotte, VA. p. 44.

3. Iowa State University F '04 Financial Report and Office of Vice Provost for Research. April 27, 2005.

4. Financial Report. 2003–2004. Northern Michigan University, Marquette, MI.

5. Rawson, Tom. 2005. Personal Correspondence. Kansas State University financial data. May 3, 2005.

6. Luft, LeRoy D. 2000. *Survey of Structure of Cooperative Extension.* University of Idaho Cooperative Extension System. March 2000.

7. Collins, Jim. 2001. *Good to Great.* Harper Business, an Imprint of Harper-Collins Publishers, New York.

8. Flawn, Peter T. 1990. *A Primer for University Presidents: Managing the Modern College and University.* University of Texas Press, Austin.(Out of print, available through UMI Books on Demand, 300 Zeb Road, Ann Arbor, MI.)

9. Ellis, Joseph J. 2001. *Founding Brothers: The Revolutionary Generation.* Alfred A. Knopf. New York.

10. Selingo, Jeffrey. 2005. *A Chronicle Survey: What Presidents Think.* The Chronicle of Higher Education. November 4, 2005.

11. American Association for the Advancement of Science. 2005. AAAS Report XXX. Research and Development. FY2006.

12. Friedman, Thomas L. 2005. *The World is Flat.* Farrar, Straus and Giroux, New York.

13. Martinson, Brian C., Melissa S. Anderson and Raymond deVries. 2005. Commentary: Scientists behaving badly. Nature 435: 737–738, June 9, 2005.

14. Regaldo, Antonio. 2005. Ethics of U.S. scientists may be shaky, Polls says. *The Wall Street Journal.* June 9, 2005. p. D4.

15. Hord, Bill. 2005. Devices facilitate student cheaters. *Omaha Sunday World Herald.* April 4, 2005. p. l.

16. Engineers Without Borders, www.engineerswithoutborders.com. November 21, 2005; Building for Keeps. *Readers Digest.* December 2005. p. 24.

17. Moffett, Matt and Geraldo Samor. 2005.Opportunity cost: In Brazil thicket of red tape spoils recipe for growth. *The Wall Street Journal.* May 25, 2005.

18. Trachtenberg, Jeffrey A. and Kevin J. Delaney. 2005. Google checks out interest in online book rental program. *The Wall Street Journal.* November 14, 2005. p. B4.

19. Perystay, Chris. 2005. In bid to globalize, U.S. colleges offer degrees in Asia. *The Wall Street Journal.* July 12, 2005. p. B1.

20. NASULGC Newsline. June 2005. p. 2.

21. Yepsen, David. 2005. Regents Face Daunting Task, Opinion Section. *Des Moines Register.* April 24, 2005.

22. Association of American Medical Colleges. 2004. *The Handbook of Academic Medicine: How Medical Schools and Teaching Hospitals Work.* 2450 N Street NW, Washington, D.C 20037.

23. Michener, James A. 1976. *Sports in America.* Random House, New York.

24. Green, Donald E. 1990. *A History of Oklahoma State University Division of Agriculture.* Published by Oklahoma State University.

25. Richter, William L. and Charles E. Reagan. 1989. *The Landon Lectures.* Published by Friends of the Library, Kansas State University, Manhattan.

26. Saltzman, Gregory M. 1998. Legal regulation of collective bargaining in colleges and universities. *The NEA 1998 Almanac of Higher Education.* p. 45–63.

27. University of Virginia Higher Education Restructuring: Background. www .virginia. edu. October 27, 2005.

28. Citizens Against Government Waste. www.cagw.org. July 24, 2005.

29. Jordan, Erin. 2005. Presidents of foundations receive above average pay. *Des Moines Register.* April 19, 2005. p. A1.

30. Kansas State University Foundation 60th Annual Report, 2005.

31. Campbell, Lynn, Erin Jordan and Madelaine Jerousek. 2005. Gift costs average at ISU, U of I. *Des Moines Register.* May 15, 2005. p. B1.

32. NASULGC NewsLine. 14: 5. May 2005.

33. Patterson, Jim. 2002. Working with governing boards. *National Association of State Universities and Land-Grant Colleges Annual Convention.* November 11, 2002.

34. Ellis, Joseph J. 2004. *His Excellency; George Washington.* Alfred A. Knopf, New York. p. 215–238.

ADDITIONAL
READINGS

Beadle, Muriel. 1972. *Where Has All the Ivy Gone?* Doubleday & Co., Inc., Garden City, New York. p. IX, X.

Budig, Gene A. 2002. *A Game of Uncommon Skill: Leading the Modern College and University.* Oryx Press, American Council on Education.

Crowley, Joseph N. 1994. *No Equal in the World: An Interpretation of the Academic Presidency.* University of Nevada Press, Reno.

Fisher, James L. and James V. Koch. 1996. *Presidential Leadership: Making a Difference.* Oryx Press, American Council on Education.

Sample, Steven B. 2002. *The Contrarian's Guide to Leadership.* Jossey-Bass, A Wiley Company, San Francisco. p. 91–105.

Shaw, Kenneth A. 1999. *The Successful President: "Buzzwords" on Leadership.* Oryx Press, American Council on Education.

INDEX

About the Author

DUANE ACKER is President Emeritus, Kansas State University, and Collaborative Professor of Animal Science, Iowa State University. He has served in various roles at five state universities as teacher, student adviser, research scientist, associate dean for instruction, dean, director of research and extension, vice chancellor, and president.